Business Result

Pre-intermediate | Teacher's Book

Mark Bartram

Class DVD worksheets by
John Hughes & Shaun Wilden

OXFORD
UNIVERSITY PRESS

Great Clarendon Street, Oxford OX2 6DP

Oxford University Press is a department of the University of Oxford.
It furthers the University's objective of excellence in research, scholarship,
and education by publishing worldwide in

Oxford   New York

Auckland Cape Town Dar es Salaam Hong Kong Karachi
Kuala Lumpur Madrid Melbourne Mexico City Nairobi
New Delhi Shanghai Taipei Toronto

With offices in

Argentina Austria Brazil Chile Czech Republic France Greece
Guatemala Hungary Italy Japan Poland Portugal Singapore
South Korea Switzerland Thailand Turkey Ukraine Vietnam

OXFORD and OXFORD ENGLISH are registered trade marks of
Oxford University Press in the UK and in certain other countries

© Oxford University Press 2009

The moral rights of the author have been asserted

Database right Oxford University Press (maker)

First published 2009
2017
18 17 16 15 14 13

All rights reserved. No part of this publication may be reproduced,
stored in a retrieval system, or transmitted, in any form or by any means,
without the prior permission in writing of Oxford University Press (with
the sole exception of photocopying carried out under the conditions stated
in the paragraph headed 'Photocopying'), or as expressly permitted by law, or
under terms agreed with the appropriate reprographics rights organization.
Enquiries concerning reproduction outside the scope of the above should
be sent to the ELT Rights Department, Oxford University Press, at the
address above

You must not circulate this book in any other binding or cover
and you must impose this same condition on any acquirer

Photocopying

The Publisher grants permission for the photocopying of those pages marked
'photocopiable' according to the following conditions. Individual purchasers
may make copies for their own use or for use by classes that they teach.
School purchasers may make copies for use by staff and students, but this
permission does not extend to additional schools or branches

Under no circumstances may any part of this book be photocopied for resale

Any websites referred to in this publication are in the public domain and
their addresses are provided by Oxford University Press for information only.
Oxford University Press disclaims any responsibility for the content

ISBN: 978 0 19 474813 1   (Book)
ISBN: 978 0 19 473943 6   (Pack)

Printed in China

This book is printed on paper from certified and well-managed sources.

ACKNOWLEDGEMENTS

Accompanying Teacher's DVD produced by: MTJ Media, Oxford, UK

*The author and publisher would like to thank the following for their kind assistance with
the accompanying Teacher's DVD*: David Grant, Judith Bolt, Cathy Rogers,
Abdullah Al-ayyaf, Mihoko Isoda, Burcu Akbaba, Jose Antonio Oroz, Geraldine
Gruchet, Kevser Çelik, Catriona Davidson (The Eckersley School of English,
Oxford, UK), Elaine Allender (British Study Centres, Oxford, UK), David
Newton (OISE, Oxford, UK), Stephanie Davis (OISE, Oxford, UK), Meriel Steele
(Oxford English Centre, Oxford, UK), Rosa Lucia (Oxford School of English,
Oxford, UK), Richard Walton (St. Clare's, Oxford, UK)

Cover photo by: Chris King

Contents

Introduction 4–7

1 Companies 8–12

2 Contacts 13–17

3 Visitors 18–22

4 New products 23–27

5 Employment 28–32

6 Customer service 33–37

7 Travel 38–42

8 Orders 43–47

9 Selling 48–52

10 New ideas 53–57

11 Entertaining 58–62

12 Performance 63–67

13 Future trends 68–72

14 Time 73–77

15 Training 78–82

16 Your career 83–87

Progress tests and Speaking tests 88–119

Teacher-Training DVD worksheets 120–125

Progress test answer key 126–129

Practice file answer key 130–134

Teacher-Training DVD worksheets answer key 135–136

Introduction

The course

Who is *Business Result* for?

Business Result is a comprehensive multi-level course in business English suitable for a wide range of learners. The main emphasis is on *enabling* your students; helping them to communicate more effectively in their working lives.

In-work students

Unlike many business English courses, *Business Result* addresses the language and communication needs of employees at all levels of an organization who need to use English at work. It recognizes that the business world is truly international, and that many people working in a modern, global environment spend much of their time doing everyday tasks in English – communicating with colleagues and work contacts by phone, via email, and in a range of face-to-face situations, such as formal and informal meetings / discussions, and various planned and unplanned social encounters. It contains topics relevant to executive-level learners, but doesn't assume that the majority of students will be international managers who 'do business' in English – the activities allow the students to participate in a way that is relevant to them, whatever their level in their company or organization.

Pre-work students

Business Result can also be used with pre-work students at college level. The course covers a variety of engaging topics over the sixteen units, so students without much work experience will receive a wide-ranging overview of the business world, as well as acquiring the key communication skills they will need in their future working lives. Each unit in this *Teacher's Book* contains suggestions for adapting the material to the needs of pre-work students.

One-to-one teaching

Many of the activities in the book are designed for use with groups of students, but they can also be easily adapted to suit a one-to-one teaching situation. Notes in the individual *Teacher's Book* units offer suggestions and help with this.

What approach does *Business Result* take?

Business Result helps students communicate in English in real-life work situations. The priority at all times is on enabling them to do so more effectively and with confidence. The target language in each unit has been carefully selected to ensure that students will be equipped with genuinely useful, transferable language that they can take out of the classroom and use immediately in the workplace.

The course recognizes that, with so many businesses now being staffed by people of different nationalities, there is an increasing trend towards using English as the language of internal communication in many organizations. As well as learning appropriate language for communicating externally – with clients or suppliers, for example – students are also given the opportunity to practise in situations that take place within an organization, such as giving a report, making arrangements, and taking part in meetings.

The main emphasis of the course is on the students speaking and trying out the target language in meaningful and authentic ways; it is expected that a large proportion of the lesson time will be spent on activating students' interest and encouraging them to talk. The material intentionally takes a communicative, heads-up approach, maximizing the amount of classroom time available to focus on and practise the target language. However, you will also find that there is plenty of support in terms of reference notes, written practice, and review material.

The syllabus is essentially communication-driven. The topics in each of the sixteen units have been chosen because of their relevance to modern business and the world of work. Vocabulary is presented in realistic contexts with reference to authentic companies or organizations. Grammar is also a key element of each unit. It is presented in an authentic context, and ensures that students pay attention to accuracy, as well as becoming more proficient at expressing themselves clearly and precisely. The *Business communication* sections ensure that students are provided with a range of key expressions they can use immediately, both in the classroom and in their day-to-day work.

Student's Book

The Student's Book pack

The *Student's Book* pack offers a blend of classroom teaching and self-study, with an emphasis on flexibility and time-efficiency. Each of the sixteen *Student's Book* units provides around four hours of classroom material with the potential for two to three hours of additional study using other components in the package.

There are no long reading texts in the units, and with an emphasis on listening and speaking, written exercises are kept to a minimum. Instead, students are directed to the *Practice file* at the back of the book. Here they will find exercises which can be used as supplementary material in class or for homework, as well as more extensive grammar notes.

Encourage your students to look at and use the *Interactive Workbook* on DVD-ROM – there are cross-references at appropriate points in each unit. Here they will find a range of self-study material to help them review, consolidate, and extend their learning.

Writing is a key feature of the course, but is not part of the main *Student's Book* units. The *Interactive Workbook* has an email writing section with exercises and model emails related to the content of every unit. There is also a writing file on the *Business Result* website.

Key features of a unit

Each unit has three main sections – *Working with words, Language at work,* and *Business communication* – dealing with core vocabulary associated with the unit theme, related grammar, and key functional expressions. Each main section ends with a short fluency task to enable students to personalize the target language. Each unit ends with a *Case study* or related *Activity*.

Unit menu

This lists the key learning objectives of the unit.

Starting point

Each unit opens with some lead-in questions to raise awareness of and interest in the unit theme. Use these questions to help you to establish what students already know about the topic and how it relates to their own working lives. They can usually be discussed as a class or in small groups.

Working with words

This first main section introduces key vocabulary in a variety of ways, including authentic reading texts, listenings, and visuals. Students are also encouraged to look at how different forms of words (verbs, adjectives, and nouns) can be built from the same root, or to look at common combinations (e.g. verb + noun, adjective + noun) that will help them to expand their personal lexicon more rapidly. This section also offers opportunities to work on your students' reading and listening skills. There is an interactive glossary of all target lexis, plus other reference vocabulary, on the *Interactive Workbook* and in PDF format on the *Business Result* website.

Language at work

The grammar is looked at from a communicative point of view; this will meet your students' expectations with regard to learning form and meaning, but also reminds them how the grammar they need to learn commonly occurs in business and work situations.

Practically speaking

This section looks at various practical aspects of everyday communication from a 'how to' perspective – for example, making polite requests, making arrangements, as well as useful social interaction, such as saying goodbye.

Business communication

This section focuses on one of five broad communication themes – meetings, presenting, exchanging information, telephoning, and socializing. These are treated differently throughout the book so that, for example, students are able to practise exchanging information on the phone as well as face to face, or compare the different language needed for giving formal and informal presentations. Typically, the section begins with students listening to an example situation (a meeting, a presentation, a social encounter, a series of phone calls). They focus on *Key expressions* used by the speakers which are listed on the page. They are then given the opportunity to practise these in various controlled and more open work-related tasks.

Case studies

Most units end with a *Case study**. This gives students an opportunity to recycle the language from the unit, demonstrate progress, and use their knowledge and ideas to resolve an authentic problem or issue. The *Case studies* have been compiled using authentic content and contexts in a way that connects with the unit theme. The content is accessible, and preparation time is minimized by including only as much information as can be assimilated relatively quickly in class. Even so, you may wish to optimize classroom time even further by asking students to read the background material before the lesson.

*Note that in five units, the *Case study* format is replaced with an *Activity* (Units 1, 3, 7, 12, and 16); this is designed to be fun and is usually presented as a game aimed at recycling the language from the unit. The *Activity* in the final unit offers students a review and further practice of language from across the sixteen units.

The *Case studies* follow a three-part structure:

Background – a short text (or texts) or listening about a real company, product, or related situation.

Discussion – two or three discussion questions on key issues arising from the background information and associated issues, providing a natural bridge to the task.

Task – a discussion, meeting simulation, or series of tasks, aimed at resolving a core issue related to the case and providing extended practice of the target language of the unit.

Tips

Short, practical tips with useful language points arising from a particular section or exercise.

Additional material

At the back of the *Student's Book*, you will find the following sections.

Practice files

This provides unit-by-unit support for your classroom work. Each file provides additional practice of target language from the three main unit sections, *Working with words, Language at work,* and *Business communication*. This can be used in two ways:

For extra practice in class – refer students to this section for more controlled practice of new vocabulary, grammar, or key expressions before moving to the next stage. The optimum point at which to do this is indicated by cross-references in the *Student's Book* unit and the teaching notes in this book.

For self-study – students can complete and self-check the exercises for review and revision outside class.

Answers for the *Practice file* appear on pages 130–134 of this book, and on the *Business Result* website.

Information files

Additional information for pair work, group activities, and *Case studies*.

Irregular verb list

Audio scripts

Interactive Workbook
DVD-ROM and online

The *Interactive Workbook* is a self-study component on DVD-ROM and online. It contains:

- interactive Exercises and Tests for each unit, with answers
- interactive Email exercises, plus a model email for each unit
- interactive Phrasebank – students can create their own personalized 'Phrasebook' (DVD-ROM only)
- interactive Glossary for students to test their vocabulary
- *Student's Book* audio in MP3 format
- a video clip for each unit with interactive exercises
- reading and discussion activities (online only).

To access the online content, students will find an access card on the inside cover of the *Student's Book*. This contains an access code to unlock the online content. Students need to go to www.oxfordlearn.com to activate their code, and then follow the instructions online to access the content.

Teacher's Book

What's in each unit?

Unit content
This provides an overview of the main aims and objectives of the unit.

Context
This section not only provides information on the teaching points covered in the unit, but also offers some background information on the main business theme of the unit, and its importance in the current business world. If you are less familiar with the world of business, you will find this section especially helpful to read before starting a unit.

Teaching notes and answers
Notes on managing the *Student's Book* exercises and various activities are given throughout, with suggested variations that you might like to try. You will find comprehensive answers to all *Student's Book* exercises, as well as notes on possible responses to discussion questions.

Extension
With some students it may be appropriate to extend an exercise in some way or relate the language point more specifically to a particular group of students. Suggestions on how to do this are given where appropriate.

Extra activity
These may present lead-in ideas – for example, a fun warm-up, comprehension questions to help clarify a particular context, or a pre-listening or reading activity if students are likely to have difficulty with a particular text or listening. Also, if you have time or would like to develop further areas of language competence, extra activities are suggested where they naturally follow the order of activities in the *Student's Book*. For example, if your students need writing practice or more confidence with speaking, extra follow-up ideas may be provided.

Alternative
With some students it may be preferable to approach an activity in a different way depending on their level or their interests. These options are provided where appropriate.

Pronunciation
Tips on teaching pronunciation and helping students improve their intelligibility are provided where there is a logical need for them. These often appear where new vocabulary is taught or for making key expressions sound more natural and fluent.

Dictionary skills
It's helpful to encourage students to use a good dictionary in class and the relevant notes suggest moments in the lesson when it may be useful to develop your students' skills in using dictionaries.

Pre-work learners
Although most users of *Business Result* will be students who are already in work, you may also be teaching classes of students who have little or no experience of the business world. Where necessary, you may want to adapt certain questions or tasks in the book to their needs, and extra notes are given for these types of learners.

One-to-one
In general, you will find that *Business Result* can be used with any size of class. However, with one-to-one students you will find that activities which have been designed with groups of students in mind will need some adaptation. In this case, you may wish to follow the suggested alternatives given in this book.

Feedback focus
Throughout the course, students are involved in speaking activities using the new language. You will want to monitor, correct, and suggest areas for improvement, as well as acknowledging successes. During and after many of the freer practice activities it will be helpful to follow the guidelines in the teaching notes on what to monitor for and ways of giving feedback.

Watch out
This is a note to highlight any potentially problematic language points, or language which students may ask about, and which has not yet been formally presented. There are suggestions on how to pre-teach certain vocabulary or clear up misunderstandings.

Photocopiable tests (pages 88–119)

There are two types of test to accompany each unit. These can be administered at the end of each unit in order to assess your students' learning and allow you, the student, or the head of training to keep track of their overall progress.

Progress test
Each of these twelve tests checks key vocabulary, grammar, and key expressions from the unit. They provide a final score out of 30. Students will need between twenty and thirty minutes to complete the test, although you can choose to set a time limit that would be appropriate for your students.

Speaking test
To help you assess communicative performance, students are given a speaking task that closely resembles one of the speaking activities in the unit. Students get a score out of a possible ten marks.

How to manage the speaking test
These are mostly set up as pair work activities in the form of role-plays or discussion (see for example *Unit 1*). There are also three speaking tests set up as a presentation, where students work alone (see *Units 10*, *15*, and *16*).

The marking criteria require students to perform five functions in the speaking test, and it is advised that you make students familiar with these criteria beforehand. You can grade each of the five stages using a straightforward scoring system of 0, 1, or 2, giving a final score out of ten. This kind of test can be carried out during the class, perhaps while other students are taking the written progress test, or you can set aside a specific time for testing.

Note that if testing is not a priority, the role-plays can also be used as extra classroom practice without necessarily making use of the marking criteria.

Teacher-Training DVD

The Teacher's Book at each level of *Business Result* is accompanied by a teacher-training *DVD* which demonstrates how sections from the *Student's Book* can be used with a typical group of students. It addresses key issues relevant to the level and looks at various classroom approaches. The *DVD* also includes commentary from teachers and one of the *Student's Book* authors, and addresses many of the questions that teachers have to ask themselves when starting a new business English course. The *Pre-intermediate DVD* uses sections from *Student's Book Unit 6*.

There are a number of different ways to use the *DVD*.

Orientation through the course
Watching the *DVD* is a fast way to familiarize yourself with the course – how the course is organized, its approach to business English, and ways of using the material in the classroom.

Supporting new teachers
If this is your first time teaching business English, you will find watching the *DVD* especially helpful. It provides guidance, advice, and tips on the difference between general English and business English, and suggests approaches to working with business English students.

Teacher development
You may be a more experienced teacher, in which case the *DVD* will address many issues you are already familiar with, but perhaps never have the opportunity to discuss with fellow professionals.

Teacher training
Directors of Studies or teacher trainers will be particularly interested in using the *DVD* as part of a complete teacher-training package. Each *DVD* forms the basis of a training session lasting approximately 45 minutes. You can use the DVD in different segments with ready-to-use worksheets (with *Answer key*) on pages 120–125 of this *Teacher's Book*, and training notes that are available from the *Business Result* website (see below). Simply photocopy the worksheets and download the training notes to use in conjunction with the *DVD* in your staff training and development sessions. Note that *DVDs* at other levels of *Business Result* address different business English themes; together, the *DVDs* from the different levels form an entire training package in teaching business English. See the website for more information.

Class DVD

The *Teacher's Book* pack also includes a DVD for use in the classroom. It includes one clip for every unit of the *Student's Book*. The clip can also be found on the *Interactive Workbook* on DVD-ROM packaged with the *Student's Book*.

You can use the DVD in class to complement your lessons. Each clip has a worksheet offering a complete lesson to accompany it. The worksheet can be downloaded from the *Class DVD*, along with an answer key and transcript.

The *Student's Book* flags up the appropriate moment to show the DVD in class with this icon: **VIDEO**

Teacher's website

The Teacher's website can be found at www.oup.com/elt/teacher/result. It contains a range of additional materials, including:

- needs analysis form – for use at the start of the course
- progress test record
- course management & assessment tools
- DVD training notes
- wordlists
- additional activities
- writing file
- reading bank.

Using the course

How to use *Business Result*

From start to finish
You can, of course, use *Business Result* conventionally, starting at *Unit 1* and working your way through each unit in turn. If you do so, you will find it works well. Each section of the unit is related thematically to the others, there is a degree of recycling and a steady progression towards overall competence, culminating in the *Case study* or final *Activity*. Timing will inevitably vary, but allow approximately four classroom hours for each unit. You will need more time if you intend to do the *Practice file* activities in class.

The 'fast-track' option
If you have less time, you can create a 'fast track' course using the *Language at work*, *Practically speaking*, and *Business communication* sections of the unit. This will still provide solid input of the core grammar that students need at this level, along with a range of useful expressions for communication in professional contexts. You should find with this option that each unit provides at least two hours of classroom material.

If your students need vocabulary support or revision, use as much of the *Working with words* section as you feel is appropriate, and refer students to the exercises in the *Practice file*.

Mix and match
If your students have more specific needs and you would like to 'cherry pick' what you feel are the most interesting and relevant sections of the book, this approach should work well. You will find that all the sections are essentially free-standing, despite being thematically linked, and can be used independently of the rest of the unit. Mix and match sections across the book to create a course that is tailored to your students' needs.

1 | Companies

Unit content

By the end of this unit, students will be able to
- describe what companies do
- talk about their company using the present simple
- make polite requests
- introduce themselves and others.

Context

The topic of *Companies* gives the students the basic initial tools for business interaction. Anybody who works or plans to work in business will need a certain amount of vocabulary for describing a company, including its main activities, its location, and its workforce. Not only is it important to find out about a contact's company for practical business reasons, but it is also a subject of interest to most business people, and so will be a topic of conversation in many business situations, including socializing.

Social interaction in business is crucial for the forging of good relationships and making new contacts. Cultural differences can lead to misunderstandings if business people do not use the correct register, tone, and degree of appropriateness.

In this unit, students will learn how to describe their companies. They will also have the opportunity to practise two important social aspects of business interaction – making polite requests and introducing themselves and others. At the end of the unit, the students will play a game that will help them practise the language studied.

Starting point

Allow the students a few seconds to look at the photos before speaking. Elicit from the students what they know about the companies. Some information they may come up with:
- what products the companies make or services they provide
- where they are based
- how many people work for them
- how long they have been in existence.

As a variation, you could ask the students to discuss the photos in pairs first, and then feed back to the class.

The other two questions can be discussed in pairs, groups, or as a class.

Working with words

NB the companies featured in the illustration are not the ones in **1**.

1 Ask students to read the five company descriptions and complete the names.

Answers
1 Yahoo   2 Michelin   3 Ikea   4 Airbus   5 Samsung

2 Ask the students to complete the sentences with words from the descriptions in **1**.

Answers
1 produce   5 is based
2 provide   6 subsidiary
3 specialize   7 sales
4 employee   8 competitor

Pronunciation

Make sure the students can pronounce the words with the correct stress. Ask them to mark the main stress.
   pro*duce*, em*ploy*ee, pro*vide*, *spec*ialize, sub*sid*iary, com*pet*itor

» If students need more practice, go to **Practice file 1** on page 102 of the **Student's Book**.

3 Students make sentences using the words in the table. Weaker classes should write the sentences; stronger classes could do it orally. They may need to ask you for some vocabulary, or consult a bilingual dictionary.

Suggested answers
Gazprom provides gas to many European countries.
Pirelli makes tyres.
AOL offers internet services and online software.
Mitsubishi specializes in electrical and electronic products.
Volkswagen produces cars and vans. Its competitors are Ford and Renault.
UNICEF (the United Nations Children's Fund) operates in more than 150 countries, and works to develop, protect, and save children.

4 01▷ Allow students time to study the table. Ask them what kind of information they need to listen for. Play the listening and students complete the table. Students can compare answers. Play the listening again.

Answers
1 Automatic
2 door
3 security
4 Swedish
5 30
6 3
7 150
8 competitors

5 Students work in pairs and talk about Assa Abloy, using information from **4**.

6 Students work in pairs with someone from another company, if possible. If students are all from the same company, follow the suggestions under 'Pre-work learners' below. You might like to provide a model first and ask students to guess the name of the company. *I work for X. We make cars. We have about 3,000 employees. We are based in Italy. Our main competitors are Porsche and Maserati. It's a subsidiary of Fiat. We specialize in sports cars, and we have sales of about €1,700 million.* (Ferrari)

Then allow students time to prepare this speaking activity. To make it more challenging for the listener, ask him / her to write notes on what his / her partner said. One or two better students could report back from their notes.

Pre-work learners
Ask students to imagine they work for a (real) well-known company or to invent a company and the relevant information.

One-to-one
You might like to talk about your school or organization first, to give your student an extra model.

ⓘ Refer students to the **Interactive Workbook Glossary** for further study.

Language at work

1 Ask students to work in pairs and to ask and answer the questions. Check they use the correct third person form to answer questions 2–4.

2 Students match the answers to the questions.

Answers
a 4   b 3   c 5   d 1   e 2

3 Students may not be familiar with an approach which asks them to find examples of a grammatical rule. You may need to guide them through this.

Watch out! Note that for students who have acquired English at work, the grammatical terminology here may be unknown. Be prepared to explain the terms *present simple*, *third person*, *singular / plural*, *verb*, and give examples.

Answers
1 It provides …
2 I have … / I do …
3 Do you work …? / … does it do … / Does it operate …?
4 Is it …?

Pre-work learners
As before, ask students to imagine they work for a (real) well-known company or to invent a company and the relevant information.

» If students need more practice, go to **Practice file 1** on page 103 of the **Student's Book**.

4 Ask the students to study the artwork next to the text. Elicit which company is being talked about (*Nestlé*). Ask them what they know about it – this will recycle the language from the unit so far. You could elicit what kind of text it is (*a website page giving information about an upcoming programme*). The students read the text and discuss the questions in pairs.

Watch out! You may need to explain the phrases *local communities* and *protect the environment*.

Tip Draw the students' attention to the *Tip*. You may like to point out that when a preposition is in end-position, it is pronounced with a stronger sound than in the middle of a sentence.

5 The students use the prompts 1–10 to make questions. They should write these, as they will need them for the following activity.

Unit 1 | Companies

9

> **Answers**
> 1 How old is the company?
> 2 What products does the company specialize in?
> 3 What are its annual sales?
> 4 Where is its head office?
> 5 How many factories does it have?
> 6 Does the company sell products in all five continents?
> 7 How many people does it employ?
> 8 What does it offer its employees?
> 9 Does the company do a lot of work in the community?
> 10 How does it protect the environment?

Feedback focus

Pay special attention to answer 9, where *do* is both the auxiliary and the main verb: this may be confusing for the students. Check the students understand the verbs *employ* in 7 and *protect* in 10.

6 02▷ Students match the questions in **5** to the answers. Then play the listening so that they can check their answers.

> **Answers**
> a 5 b 1 c 6 d 7 e 3 f 8 g 9 h 2 i 4 j 10

7 Stronger classes may be able to do this exercise orally. Weaker students should write the sentences. As this is an accuracy exercise, you should insist on a fairly high level of correctness, especially with the present simple verb forms.

> **Answers**
> 1 The company is more than 140 hundred years old.
> 2 It specializes in food and beverages.
> 3 Its annual sales are more than 107 billion Swiss francs.
> 4 Its head office is in Vevey, Switzerland.
> 5 It has 780 factories.
> 6 The company sells in all five continents.
> 7 It employs 276,000 people.
> 8 It offers many possibilities for training.
> 9 It gives money and other help to the community.
> 10 It protects the environment by using less water, energy, and packaging.

8 Students work in pairs and ask and answer the questions from **5** about each other's companies. You may need to help with vocabulary, especially for questions 8–10, where the students may need to use vocabulary different from that of the listening text. Students should note down the answers in preparation for **9**.

Pre-work learners

As before, ask students to imagine they work for a (real) well-known company; or to invent a company and the relevant information.

9 Put the students in new pairs. They should report to their new partner about the first partner's company. Make sure they use the third person forms correctly.

Dictionary activity

Write the following list of words from this section on the board: *company, operate, work, service, head, sale, preserve, environment*. Students look up the words in a good monolingual dictionary. How many different meanings does the dictionary give for each word? Which meaning is the one in this section? (NB the answers will depend on the particular dictionary they use.) Students could compare different dictionaries to see which give more meanings.

Practically speaking

This section focuses on two types of request: asking if the speaker can do something (permission) and asking the other person to do something. *Would* can only be used for the second of these. *Would* is more polite / formal than *could* which in turn is more polite / formal than *can*. *Could* is appropriate in most situations.

1 The students complete the questions with *I* or *you*.

> **Answers**
> 1 I   2 you   3 I   4 you   5 you   6 you

2 03▷ Students first match the questions in **1** to the responses a–f, then listen to check. They then practise the conversations in pairs.

Pronunciation

Intonation is very important in making requests. Flat intonation with no ups and downs can sound rude. Use the model on the audio for the students to imitate.

> **Answers**
> 1 b or d   2 f   3 e   4 c   5 a   6 b or d

3 Make sure the students respond appropriately, using the models in **2**.

Suggested answers
1 Can / Could I have your telephone number? Yes, of course, it's (667654).
2 Could you give me your address? Certainly. It's 39 Green Street, …
3 Could / would you speak more slowly, please? Yes, of course.
4 Could you sign this document? Sure.
5 Can I take these chairs? Yes, of course.
6 Could I talk to you later? Sorry, I'm really busy later.
7 Can I borrow your pen? Yes, of course.
8 Could you say that again? Yes, sorry. I said …

Pronunciation

Students should be encouraged to pronounce *can* with a weak form /kən/. The stress should go on the main verb. For *could*, the 'l' is not sounded.

Tip Refer students to the *Tip* about *can*, *could*, and *would*.

Business communication

1 04▷ Introduce the topic of introducing yourself. Teach the phrase *introduce yourself*. Elicit from the students typical topics of conversation for this situation (*nationality / origin, job, reason for being here*).

Make sure students know the names of the two speakers. Play the listening once only. Stress to the students that they do not need to understand every word, just find the answers to the three questions. Students work in pairs and compare their answers.

Answers
1 Czech
2 journalist
3 She's here to research an article (on Internet service providers)

2 05▷ The students complete the dialogue. If the students are really struggling, you could write the answers on the board in the wrong order and ask them to choose.

Answers
1 Is
2 introduce
3 too, from
4 who
5 do
6 why
7 you, him
8 again
9 This

Alternative
Write the key words from the dialogue on the board or an overhead transparency. Students should enact the dialogue using only the prompts e.g. *me / Is / free* ?
You can add or take away prompts according to how well they are doing.

3 05▷ Play the conversation again and ask students to match Gianluca's questions to Jana's responses. Before they listen, check they understand the task: they do not need to write down the questions. Once you have checked the correct answers, students work in pairs and practise the dialogue.

Answers
2 d   3 h   4 f   5 a   6 e   7 g   8 b

4 Students discuss this question briefly in pairs.

Possible answer
Because Gianluca asks all the questions. / Because Jana isn't very interested in him and doesn't try to find out about him.

5 06▷ Ask the students to listen to the new conversations and answer the questions. Point out that *What about* + noun is a useful way of repeating a question with a new focus without having to repeat the whole question.

Answers
1 That he is a sales manager and that he is at the conference to find new customers in the European market.
2 1 What about you? What do you do?
  2 What about you? What are you here for?

Pronunciation

Ask why the stress in Jana's questions is on the word *you* whereas it wasn't in Gianluca's. (*Jana is repeating back the same questions, but changing whom they refer to.*)

» If students need more practice, go to **Practice file 1** on page 102 of the **Student's Book**.

6 Ask the students to practise the questions in **5** before they start **6**. In particular, make sure they stress *you* in all cases. For **6**, allow students time to prepare their conversations. Be careful about *company* – the students may be tempted to reply 'What are you?' rather than 'What do you do?'

Feedback focus

When you feed back on this activity, point out some examples of both correct and incorrect stress (without necessarily naming names) that you heard.

One-to-one

Make sure the student plays the B role at some stage.

---

7 Draw your students' attention to *Key expressions* and practise them together.

Divide the students into groups of four or five. Set the scene (a party at the conference). Elicit why such parties are an important part of business life (*they are a good chance to make new contacts*).

Students could have a new identity on a role card or invent one themselves to make it more interesting, especially if they work for the same company. Students stand up and wander around as if at a party where they do not know anybody. You could tell them they have to make three new friends / contacts. In addition, they have to introduce their new friends to a third person if possible.

Feedback focus

Give some feedback about their language performance. Correct one or two common errors, but do not overdo it.

One-to-one

You could take the roles of several different people at the party, and your student must introduce him / herself to you over and over again.

ⓘ Refer students to the **Interactive Workbook Email** and **Phrasebank** sections for further study and to **Exercises and Tests** for revision.

Activity

Background

The objective of this game is to practise the language for this unit in a light-hearted context.

Procedure

The rules of the game, which are in File 01 on page 135 of the Student's Book, are fairly self-explanatory. Check your students understand the rules. You could ask them to have a trial run of one or two 'goes' each, just to make sure.

07▷ Note that the questions for the 'Joker' squares are both on the audio and on page 147 of the Student's Book. However, since the pairs will be playing at different speeds, and reaching these squares at different moments, it will probably be easier for them to call you over and for you simply to read out the questions. An alternative would be to give the Joker questions to one of each group to read out (and the answers).

Answers to Joker questions
1 Google
2 Rolls-Royce
3 Sony
4 Boeing
5 Pirelli
6 Nokia
7 Danone

One-to-one

To make sure that the student gets the maximum practice in the language on the board, give them the chance to answer first each time. If they answer correctly on their turn, they proceed as per the normal rules. If they answer correctly on your turn, you must stay in the same place.

» Unit 1 **Progress test** and **Speaking test**, pages 88–89.

2 | Contacts

Unit content

By the end of this unit, students will be able to
- describe their job and the people they work with
- talk about work activities using the present continuous
- give phone numbers and spell names
- make or receive a simple telephone call.

Context

The topic of this unit *Contacts* will be relevant to all business people. Making contact with people within your company or outside is an essential part of business life as an increasing number of tasks are outsourced, companies use more sub-contractors, and employees have an increasing amount of contact with customers and suppliers. Much of this interaction involves exchanging information and ideas, and giving support, and is carried out on the phone. Indeed, some jobs are conducted virtually 100% on the phone. However, doing business over the phone in a foreign language without the aid of facial expressions can lead to misunderstandings and, therefore, lost business.

In this unit, students learn how to talk about their job both in terms of what it involves and current activities. The unit also deals with some of the set phrases needed in English to talk on the phone effectively. Finally, students will have the chance to discuss corporate strategy and how to deal with a public relations crisis. A company can have a PR crisis at any time and it will usually be totally unexpected.

Starting point

Allow the students time to consider their responses to the questions.

Pre-work learners

Ask students to think of a job they have seen being done (e.g. shop assistant, hotel receptionist), and imagine the answers to the exercise.

Extension

Students make a chart of how often they speak to their colleagues. They draw three or four concentric circles. They then write the names of colleagues on the circles according to how often they talk to them: near the centre of the circles for colleagues they talk to a lot and then further out for others they talk to only occasionally. In pairs, they then exchange charts and ask each other about the charts.
This could be an opportunity to revise adverbs of frequency:
  A *How often do you talk to Juan Rodriguez?*
  B *Once a week, sometimes twice a week. He's my area manager.*

Working with words

1 Write the three jobs on the board. Check the pronunciation, particularly *psychologist*. Explain *retail* and its antonym *wholesale* if necessary. Ask the students to say what the three jobs are.

> **Possible answers**
> **Retail buyer:** a person who buys goods or services for a shop
> **Public relations officer:** the person inside a company who deals with the public image of the company, media relations, etc.
> **Occupational psychologist:** a person working for or with a company who studies and tries to improve the working relationships and behaviour of the personnel to make the company more effective and / or increase job satisfaction

2 Students read the text and compare their answers in pairs.

Dictionary activity

Make sure the students have access to a good business English dictionary (for example, the Oxford Business English Dictionary). The students should use the dictionary to find or check the correct definitions. NB some of the words will be cognates (words which have the same origin in different languages, e.g. *journalist, colleagues*), but the students should check these anyway in case they are false friends (words which look the same but have a different meaning).

3 Students read the text again and complete the table.

Answers

Which person or people …	Sara	Benjamin	Heidi
work(s) on problems of communication?		✓	✓
work(s) with people outside the company?	✓	✓	✓
work(s) with products?	✓		
works with companies, but not for a company?			✓

Watch out! We use *work for a company* when we are actually employed by that company. We use *work with a company* when we have dealings with another company, or we are self-employed and work at their site for a limited period.

4 Students find the words and phrases in the text in italics and match them to definitions a–h.

Answers
a suppliers
b employment agencies
c subcontractors
d colleagues
e training organizations
f consultant
g customers
h staff

Pronunciation

Write the word *company* on the board with its three syllables (*com – pa – ny*). Explain that the first syllable has the stronger stress: <u>com</u>pany. Students then put the other words into groups of the same stress pattern.
Answers
su<u>pp</u>liers, con<u>sul</u>tant, em<u>ploy</u>ment
<u>jour</u>nalists, <u>a</u>gencies, <u>cus</u>tomers
<u>coll</u>eagues, <u>train</u>ing
subcon<u>trac</u>tors
organi<u>za</u>tions

5 Students work in pairs to find out about the other student's company. Encourage the students to ask questions, e.g.
Do you have contact with customers in your job?
Does your company use training organizations?

Pre-work learners

Students think of a job they might do in the future or a job they know something about and imagine which people or organizations they have contact with.

6 08▷ Before listening, ask what *software* is. Make sure students understand the vocabulary and the task. You could ask them what a person working in a software company might do and who might be involved.

Watch out! You might need to pre-teach the following. In the chart: *sales rep* = someone who travels to different places trying to persuade people to buy their company's products or services
In the recording: *technical issue* = a technical subject or problem that people are thinking or worried about; *bug* = a mistake or a problem in a computer program

Answers
The following should be ticked:
People: customers, sales reps, programmers
Jobs: answering calls, visiting, discussing old programs

7 08▷ Refer the students to the words in bold in the text on page 12. Students complete the description of Sang Chun's job using each phrase once.

Answers
Main job: consists of, involves
Other tasks: involved in, takes part
Typical problems: deals with

Tip Refer students to the *Tip* about structures with verb / adjective + preposition + *-ing*.

Extension

Students complete the following sentences with an appropriate verb in the *-ing* form to make a sentence which is true for them:
1 I'm interested in …
2 I'm very fond of …
3 I've never been very keen on …
4 I'm really good at …
Students then work in pairs to see if they have answers in common. Encourage the use of follow-up questions which are good for small talk.
A *I'm really good at skiing.*
B *Oh really? Do you go skiing often?*

» If students need more practice, go to **Practice file 2** on page 104 of the **Student's Book**.

8 Students think alone about the things in the list and then discuss the answers in pairs. Students could give very short presentations using their information.

ⓘ Refer students to the **Interactive Workbook Glossary** for further study.

Language at work

1 Students answer the questions. Make sure they do not make mistakes with the present simple and continuous, e.g.
   * *I am working for a big company in Berlin.*
   * *This week I work on a big project in Turkey.*

2 Students match the answers to the questions.

   Watch out! You might need to teach the verb *get* (in answer a) to mean *deliver* or *send*.

   Answers
   a 2   b 1   c 3

3 Students may not be familiar with the grammatical terminology here, so you may need to briefly review the forms of these two tenses.

   Answers
   1 present continuous   3 present simple
   2 present continuous

4 Students complete the form of the present continuous.

   Answer
   to be

5 Students work in pairs, and discuss where they might see the four signs.

   Answers
   a on a lift (elevator) which is not working
   b on a computer screen when the user has keyed in the wrong password
   c on the door of a room where a meeting is taking place
   d on an email (automated reply)

6 09▷ Before listening, you could ask students to listen only for key words and match them to the signs. Play the conversations just once.

   Answers
   1 sign b   2 sign c

Feedback focus

Ask the students why they chose the signs they did and which words helped them. This will show weaker students how to use key words to reconstruct the gist of a conversation.
Suggested answers
1 access, files, computer, password, server
2 problem, meeting, disturbing, room, waiting

7 09▷ Check students understand the verbs. Students read the dialogue and complete it with the present continuous form of the verbs. Then play the listening again and students check their answers. NB you will need to pause the recording after Conversation 1 ready for Exercise 8.

   Answers
   A Who **am** I **speaking** to?
   B Sorry, this is Nadira. **I'm trying** to access my customer files, but the computer **isn't accepting** my password.
   A … There's a problem with the server.
   B **Is** somebody **working** on it at the moment?
   A Yes, *I* am. But it's not easy, because I'm on my own here. Everybody else **is having** lunch.

8 09▷ Play conversation 2 again. Explain to the students that they do not have to reproduce the conversation word for word, just in a general sense with the correct grammar.

   Answers
   See audio 09 on page 148 of the Student's Book.

» If students need more practice, go to **Practice file 2** on page 105 of the **Student's Book**.

9 Allow time for students to prepare the questions. Make sure that they have used the correct present form. Students then work in pairs and ask and answer the questions.

   Answers
   Do you speak English at work?
   Do you travel a lot for your work?
   Are you travelling anywhere this week?
   Do you sometimes work on special projects?
   Are you doing any other training courses at the moment?
   Are you receiving any visitors this week?
   Does your boss work every day?
   Is he or she working today?
   Does he or she travel a lot for work?
   Is he or she travelling this week?

Pre-work learners

Students could use their invented jobs from exercise 5 in *Working with words* above or talk about their current course of study, their school / college, or about a teacher.

Feedback focus

Monitor for correct use of the present simple or continuous, and use of the *does* auxiliary or third person 's' in the present simple.

ⓘ Refer students to the **Interactive Workbook Email** section for further study.

Unit 2 | Contacts

Practically speaking

Tip Refer students to the *Tip* about how phone numbers are said in English.

1 10▷ Students listen and write the phone numbers.

> **Answers**
> 1 0044
> 2 07700 900347

Extension

Rapid number dictation: students will often be in situations where they are expected to write down phone numbers quickly. Ask students to write down the following numbers which you should say at normal, or near normal, speed.
1 oh one six three two, nine six oh, oh one three five (01632 960 0135)
2 seven double six, seven two seven (766727)
3 oh double seven double oh, nine double oh six eight nine (07700 900 689)
4 oh two oh, seven nine four six, oh five double four (020 7946 0544)
5 extension five one double seven (5177)
6 oh one nine one, four nine eight, six double eight (0191 498 688)

2 The students should do this activity without writing down their numbers first!

3 11▷ You may want to check students' knowledge of the English alphabet first. Often these pairs of letters are confused: g / j; a / e; j / y; b / p; v / w.

The students listen and write the names.

> **Answers**
> 1 Geoff Eccleston
> 2 Briony Rhys

4 If the students are pre-work, they should spell the name of their school or college, or the street where they live.

Business communication

1 12▷ Ask the students to read through the questions carefully. Tell students to only listen for the key vocabulary. Students listen to the conversations and answer the questions.

> **Answers**
> 1 a 2 b 1
> 2 1 to offer the customer a special discount on printers
>   2 to offer (Leo) some work

2 12▷ Students match the questions to the responses. They then listen to conversation 1 again and check their answers.

> **Answers**
> 1 c 2 a 3 b 4 e 5 d

3 12▷ Play conversation 1 again. Students decide which sentences and responses are said by the caller and which by the receiver. NB you will need to pause the recording after Conversation 1 ready for Exercise 5.

> **Answers**
> 1 caller; c receiver
> 2 receiver; a caller
> 3 receiver; b caller
> 4 caller; e receiver
> 5 receiver; d caller

4 Students work in pairs and take turns to be the caller and the receiver. Students can invent the details of names, products, and prices.

5 12▷ Allow time for students to study the table. Ask them to make five questions. Weaker classes should write the questions alone, then compare in pairs. Stronger classes could say the questions in open class. The students then listen again to the second conversation, and check their answers. They also write down the responses to the questions. You may want to play the conversation more than once.

> **Answers**
> Could I speak to Leo Keliher, please? Response: I'm afraid he's out of the office at the moment.
> Could I leave a message? Response: Yes, of course.
> Could I have your name, please? Response: This is Natalie Kent.
> Could you ask Leo to call me back? Response: Yes, sure.
> Could you tell me what it's about? Response: Yes, I'm phoning to offer him some subcontracting work.

Watch out! Note that the last question is an indirect question and so the word order is similar to a statement, not a question.

» If students need more practice, go to **Practice file 2** on page 104 of the **Student's Book**.

6 Students work in groups of three. Allow a few minutes for them to think about the language they will need. Students might need to refer to the *Key expressions*. They then role-play the conversations. Go round to all the groups and monitor carefully, making a note of common mistakes. When they have finished, they can swap roles and have the conversations again.

Feedback focus
Monitor for correct use of the phrases from exercise 1, including natural stress, rhythm, and polite intonation.

One-to-one
The student could play the A role, while you play B and C; then change over and you play A, while he / she plays B and C.

ⓘ Refer students to the **Interactive Workbook Phrasebank** for further study and to **Exercises and Tests** for revision.

Case study
Background
This *Case study* presents a situation where a company encountered a major problem with its products. In public relations terms, this could mean the end of the company, or at least have a big impact on its market share. However, through a combination of excellent crisis management and shrewd use of the media to get its message across to the customers, it managed to avert a major crisis, and re-build market share within a short period. So effective was the company's management of this crisis that it has become (literally) a textbook example of how to behave in such a situation.

The *Task* is in two parts: the first involves the students making a phone call and in the second, they work in small groups to resolve a similar problem to the *Case study*.

As a lead-in, ask the students if they can think of situations which a company might encounter that could lead to some kind of major problem or crisis for the company. Examples might be: a strike by all the employees; some kind of explosion or fire affecting a product.

Students then read the text entitled *Crisis? What crisis?*

Watch out! In order for students to understand the text in detail, you may need to pre-teach: *pharmaceutical, contaminated, cyanide poison*.

Discussion
The questions can be discussed in open class, or in small groups. Then ask students to read File 02 on page 135 of the Student's Book.

Watch out! Possibly problematic vocabulary items in File 02: *warn, recalled, packaging*.

Task
1 Make sure students know what a *moisturizer* is. Set up the telephone calls carefully. You should explain that Student A always plays the same role, that of the area manager for the cosmetics company, while Student B has two different roles, first as the personal assistant to the production manager, and then as the journalist.

2 You might want to group strong, confident students together, and more timid students together, otherwise the confident ones will tend to dominate. You could ask students to take minutes and then give a formal report – either written or oral – to the rest of the class, or to newly formed groups.

One-to-one
For the telephone calls, you should play the part of Student B. For the discussion, make sure you let the student talk for the majority of the time. Ask them to give a report to you of what you have discussed (this could be a homework writing task).

» Unit 2 **Progress test** and **Speaking test**, pages 90–91.

3 | Visitors

Unit content

By the end of this unit, students will be able to
- talk about company structure
- ask questions
- welcome visitors
- present visual information.

Context

Visitors are a key element in business life. First of all, the visitor may be a potential investor or partner, or a new or regular supplier or client. Secondly, in these days of globalization and multinational companies, the visitor may work for the same company or a subsidiary. Thirdly, the trend, nowadays in business, is to encourage as many employees as possible to get out and meet customers and clients.

As part of a visit, someone may be taken around a company to visit the different departments. It is important for the visitor to be able to ask questions about these departments and the people who work in them, and for the host to be able to answer them. Moreover, for the host, making your visitor feel comfortable by making small talk may well contribute to the success of their visit.

In addition, giving a clear coherent presentation about your company or organization may be part of this visit, but it is also a skill which many business people have to transfer to other business situations, for example, conferences.

In this unit, students will focus on the departments in a company and what people in those departments do. Students will also have plenty of question practice both in asking about company structure and making visitors feel welcome. Finally, they will learn how to use visuals in a presentation.

Starting point

Ask the students to work in groups of three. They discuss questions 1–2 and make a list together for question 3.

Allow the students time to consider their responses to the questions and compare their answers with a partner, before feeding back to the rest of the class.

Pre-work learners

Make the questions hypothetical:
1 Why might people visit other companies?
2 Imagine you worked in the Research and Development department. Who might visit your department?

Feedback focus

Be prepared to spend a certain amount of time on question 3. Different companies have different departments, and their names will differ as well. Students may know the name of a department only in their own language, so either you will have to translate for them, or, more usefully, get them to explain what the department does, and then feed in the English vocabulary.

Working with words

1 You might want to write the title of the text on the board and check the meaning. Ask why customer contact is important and who usually does it.

Students should read the questions before they read the text. This gives a purpose to their reading.

Extra activity

Students predict 5–10 words they think will be in the article. As they read, they tick off the ones they predicted successfully.

You might want to give a time limit of three minutes to encourage quicker reading.

Answers
1 to listen and learn (from customers)
2 The teams included people from different departments.
3 R+D, Marketing, Sales
4 Yes. It increased customer satisfaction and it gave staff ideas for changing the products or services offered to customers.

2 Students read the text again and answer the questions.

Answers
1 sales
2 marketing
3 R+D
4 technical support
5 customer service

3 You may need to pre-teach the vocabulary in the list. Check pronunciation, including the different ways of pronouncing the third person 's':
/z/ finds buys maintains deals
/s/ checks
/ɪz/ arranges organizes.

Ask the students to complete the sentences using the verbs.

Answers	
2 organizes	5 maintains
3 buys	6 deals
4 finds	7 checks

Pronunciation

Check word stress on the department names:
<u>Lo</u>gistics   <u>Training</u>   <u>Purchasing</u>   Human Re<u>sources</u>
<u>Finance</u>   <u>Quality Control</u>

4 This is an activity to help students to remember the vocabulary in **3**. Student B could be asked to close their book. Insist on a good level of pronunciation.

5 13▷ This activity helps reinforce the department names from **3**. The students listen to the conversations and complete the table. Play the listening once.

Answers
Person 1 works in Finance. Her visitor works in IT.
Person 2 works in Logistics. His visitor works in Purchasing.
Person 3 works in Training. Her visitor works in Human Resources.

Extension

For weaker students, you could make one of these three extracts into a dictation. Play the extract in short chunks of no more than five words, stopping in logical places. The students write down exactly what they hear. Play the extract three times, and then students check what they have written against the audio script.

Watch out! You might need to pre-teach the following.
do reports, It takes a (really) long time, I have a meeting, financial reporting, the whole group, international transporters, a small number of suppliers, marketing software, special training needs, offer courses

6 13▷ Students listen again and complete the sentences.

Answers	
1 responsible for	4 have contact with
2 divided into	5 report to
3 charge of	

» If students need more practice, go to **Practice file 3** on page 106 of the **Student's Book.**

7 Students work in pairs and ask and answer the questions. Remind students that prepositions often come at the end of a question in English (see Unit 1). The stress often comes on the word before the preposition:
Who do you rep<u>or</u>t to?

Pre-work learners

Student's can invent their own identity or give them these role cards:

A
Department: HR
Responsible for: arranging interviews
Department head: Jean Renoir
Report to: Lucy Tanner
Contact with: Training
Divided into:
3 sections: – new staff
– Health and Safety
– contracts

B
Department: Finance
Responsible for: paying invoices
Department head: Mr Lin
Report to: Mrs Pastellas
Contact with: Purchasing
Divided into:
4 sections: – salaries
– invoices and billing
– accounts
– legal

Photocopiable © Oxford University Press

8 Students work in pairs. They take turns to describe their job and department, and other people and departments around them. You might want to ask them to discuss similarities and differences.

Unit 3 | Visitors

19

Pre-work learners

Ask the students to describe the departments of the school / college where they learn.

One-to-one

Describe your own school or training organization, and exchange information with your student.

ⓘ Refer students to the **Interactive Workbook Glossary** for further study.

Language at work

1 You could start by eliciting all the question words they know. It might be useful at this point to distinguish between open or *Wh-* questions, which start with a question word like *What?* or *Who?*, and closed or *Yes / No* questions.

Refer students to the *Tip*. Then students write a suitable question word (or words) in each question.

Answers
1 How many
2 When (Why / How long ago are also possible)
3 Which
4 How
5 What

2 Students complete the table with the questions from **1**. Make sure students know what the different parts of the table mean, e.g. *auxiliary verb* and *rest of question*.

Answers

Question word or phrase	Auxiliary verb	Subject	Main verb	Rest of question
2 When	did	your company	open	in your town?
3 Which department	do	you	work in?	
4 How often	do	visitors	come	to your company?
5 What	are	you	working on	at the moment?

3 14▷ Ask students to look at the photo and say what is happening (*an employee is showing a visitor round*). You might want to ask students to write down the key words they used to get their answers.

Answers
1 CEO's office
2 HR Manager
3 Call centre
4 Alex Fenton

4 Students write out the questions in full to practise question word order.

Answers
1 How often does he use this office?
2 Where does he come from?
3 How long are you staying here?
4 Who do you want to see while you're here?
5 When did it open?
6 How many calls do you receive a day? / How many calls a day do you receive?
7 Which countries do you visit?
8 How much do you know about the Polish market?

Extension

For stronger students you could copy out the slashed sentences, but with one word missing, e.g.
this / often / use / How / office / he ? (omitting 'does')
Students have to order the sentences and suggest the missing word.
Suggested omissions
2 does 3 are 4 to 5 it 6 many 7 Which 8 the

Pronunciation

Usually intonation on questions with a question word will go down.

5 14▷ Students match the questions in **4** to answers a–h, then listen to the answers and check.

Answers
1 g 2 f 3 e 4 a 5 b 6 h 7 c 8 d

» If students need more practice, go to **Practice file 3** on page 107 of the **Student's Book**.

6 You might want to elicit these questions first. Explain that there is a new employee in the company. Ask students to suggest what questions they might have on their first day. Students then use the prompts to make questions.

Watch out! For number 6, students may wish to ask a subject question:
How many people work for this company?
Explain that when the answer to the question is the subject of the sentence, e.g.
10,000 people (work for this company)
we do not use the auxiliary verbs *do / does / did*.

Suggested answers
1 Who is (the person) in charge of this department?
2 What are the opening and closing hours? / When does the office open / close?
3 Where are the nearest toilets?
4 What time is lunch? / How much time do I have for lunch?
5 Where is the photocopier?
6 How many people does the company employ? / How many people work in this company / department?
7 Do I need a key or security pass? / Where do I get a key or security pass?
8 What time are the coffee or tea breaks? / Are there any coffee or tea breaks?

7 Students work in pairs and ask and answer the questions about their departments.

Pre-work learners

Students should invent the information or talk about their school / college, etc.

Practically speaking

1 15▷ Before listening, you could ask students what kind of questions they might ask visitors to welcome them to their company. Students complete the sentences using phrases from the list. Then they listen and check.

Watch out! Note that question 5 refers to the whole length of the stay, including the future – this is not to be confused with 'How long have you been here?' which asks about 'up till now'.

Answers
1 Welcome
2 Did you have
3 Did you find
4 Where
5 How long
6 Would you like
7 Did you get

2 15▷ The students listen again and write the responses. Then they practise the conversations.

Pronunciation

Students should pay attention to the stress and intonation of both questions and answers, as they clearly want to make a good impression on their visitor or host by sounding interested and / or enthusiastic. (Flat intonation tends to signal boredom in English.) Ask them to repeat the models in the listening if necessary.

Answers
1 Thanks very much. It's nice to be here.
2 Yes, thanks. It was fine.
3 No problem. Your secretary sent me a very good map.
4 At the Continental Hotel.
5 Just three days.
6 Yes, please. A coffee would be nice.
7 Yes, I did thanks.

3 16▷ Students listen and then complete the follow-up questions. You might want to add that we make follow-up comments or questions when we answer questions too.
A *Did you have a good trip?*
B *Yes, thanks. The plane was a bit late, but everything else was fine.*

They could compare answers in pairs before feeding back. Play the listening again if necessary.

Answers
1 your first time
2 did you arrive
3 get here
4 comfortable enough
5 to look
6 like it
7 make any

4 Students work in pairs and have a conversation using the questions in **1** and the follow-up questions in **3**. Check the pronunciation of *comfortable* (with just three syllables). You could ask them to close their books and give them one- or two-word prompts to see if they can remember.
T *What time …*
S *… did you arrive last night?*

Extra activity

You could make this more realistic by making the classroom the reception of a company. Students stand up and take turns to be the host and the visitor.

ⓘ Refer students to the **Interactive Workbook Email** section for further study.

Business communication

1 Ask the students what they know about Lenovo (*Chinese computer manufacturer*). Students look at the three slides. Encourage stronger students to explain roughly what the slides show. Do not correct students at the moment.

Watch out! You may need to pre-teach the following items: *rise, fall, market share, breakdown, key figures, organizational structure*. Items which appear in **3** below should not be pre-taught.

Unit 3 Visitors

21

> **Answers**
> 1 a Slide 3 b Slide 2 c Slide 1
> 2 a Slide 2 b Slide 1 c Slide 3

2 17▷ Allow students time to study the slides, and especially the gaps. You could elicit from them the kind of information which is missing. *(Slides 1 and 2: areas and percentages; Slide 3: numbers).* Students listen once and complete the missing information.

> **Answers**
> 1 27.6
> 2 37.5
> 3 35.8
> 4 36.1
> 5 5
> 6 3,000

3 17▷ Students work in pairs and match sentence to slides. The phrases in italics are the focus of **4**, so do not work on them at this point.

> **Answers**
> a 1 b 3 c 2 d 3 e 2 f 1 g 1

4 Ask students to divide the phrases into these two categories. You may need to recap the difference between *gives you / shows / summarizes*.

> **Answers**
> 1 a, c, d   2 b, e, f, g

5 Allow students time to look at the phrases in **3** before they cover them. Students describe the slides and then say what is important about the information.

Alternative
Put some of the words in sentences a–g on the board as prompts or the 'listener' can uncover the phrases in **3** and correct the 'presenter' if they make any mistakes.

One-to-one
Ask your student to describe all three slides or you describe the slides with mistakes and your student must correct you.

» If students need more practice, go to **Practice file 3** on page 106 of the **Student's Book**.

6 Draw your students' attention to *Key expressions* and practise them together.

Students work in pairs and present 'their' slide to their partner. Encourage students to make it into a game where points are given for every piece of language from **3** that they use.

Feedback focus
Give positive feedback on their presentations, and also point out frequent mistakes. You could ask them how they felt about their presentations, and how they could be improved.

ⓘ Refer students to the **Interactive Workbook Phrasebank** for further study and to **Exercises and Tests** for revision.

Activity
Work through the rules of the game with the students. Emphasize that the aim is to ask more questions than their partner, but that their questions must be natural in the context.

Students can take turns to be the host and the visitor. However, if you are short of time, you may wish them to take turns after each new place, in order to give each student the chance to be both host and visitor.

To make the game more difficult, you can impose the rule that only grammatically correct sentences win a point. (Students will have to agree between them if a question is correct or not.)

Emphasize the rule that any question word left unused will result in the deduction of points. This will stop them using the same ones over and over again.

» Unit 3 **Progress test** and **Speaking test**, pages 92–93.

4 | New products

Unit content

By the end of this unit, students will be able to
- describe the stages in the development of a new product
- talk about new products and services using the past simple
- show interest
- give a report.

Context

The topic of this unit *New products* is important in the business world. In a technological age, products and services are constantly being developed. As soon as, or even before, one product or service is launched, another one is being initiated. People all over a company may be involved in this product or service development either as part of a cross-functional team which takes the new product through all the stages or concentrating on one stage only. Equally, business people always need to keep up with and be aware of new developments and, in any case, they are consumers themselves.

Developing any new product or service involves a considerable degree of risk. However, some of the greatest products and services of the last 100 years have been produced by entrepreneurs who have been prepared to take these risks and accept accountability for their creations. Without this entrepreneurship, such important developments such as the Internet, mobile phones, and Hotmail may not have been created.

In this unit, students have the opportunity to talk about product or service development, and to use the past simple to talk about products and services which have been created in the past by entrepreneurs. They also have practice in giving a report, which is a useful skill in the modern world. The medium for this is increasingly a visual one, as business people often do not have time to read through lengthy written reports. The information needs to be synthesized quickly and presented in a brief and memorable way.

Starting point

Allow time for students to consider their responses to the questions. Then they work in pairs and discuss the questions.

Working with words

1 18▷ The students look at the photo. Ask them what they know about *Fat Face*. If they don't know the brand, ask them to guess what kind of clothes they are from the photo. The students read the questions, then listen to the interview and answer them. Play the listening twice.

> **Answers**
> 1 In a bar (in a ski resort called Meribel in the French Alps)
> 2 Because they needed money to pay for their skiing
> 3 In the UK
> 4 It is named after a ski slope in Val d'Isere ('La Face')
> 5 Practical and stylish

2 18▷ Pre-teach the term *flow chart*. Elicit what this one shows. You could use this phase to revise the language of visual presentation from Unit 3, e.g.
This flow chart shows / summarizes the development of Fat Face.

Check the students understand the words in the list. Then ask the students to complete the chart. They listen again and check their answers.

> **Answers**
> 1 Have the original idea
> 3 Design the product
> 5 Brand the product

Watch out! Teach *brand* (verb), *trials*, and *launch*.

3 The students discuss the question in pairs. Make sure the students use the phrases from **2**.

> **Suggested answers**
> 1 You have the original idea to have something to sell!
> 2 You do market research to find out what products the public wants or needs.
> 3 You design the product to make it attractive to the public.
> 4 You do product trials to check that the product works.
> 5 You brand the product so that the public recognizes and remembers it.
> 6 You launch the product to introduce the new product to the market.

4 Students should do this exercise without using dictionaries.

> **Answers**
> 1 c   2 a   3 d   4 b

Unit 4 New products

23

5 Refer students to the *Tip*. Students match the words to the definitions. They may need a dictionary for this.

Answers
1 d **2** a **3** g **4** f **5** c **6** b **7** h **8** e

Dictionary activity
Write the two lists below on the board. Students use a good monolingual dictionary to match the words from List A to those in List B to make eight new compound adjectives. They then write sentences to illustrate the meanings.
List A: *air, low, second, long, last, world, interest, brand*
List B: *class, new, minute, conditioned, free, lasting, paid, famous*
Answers: *air-conditioned, low-paid, second-class, long-lasting, last-minute, world-famous, interest-free, brand-new*

Pronunciation
Ask students to underline the word stress on the following words.
   pra*ctical* eco*no*mical a*ttrac*tive *func*tional *sty*lish
   user-*friend*ly *well*-de*signed* com*pact* or *com*pact

» If students need more practice, go to **Practice file 4** on page 108 of the **Student's Book**.

6 Allow time for students to think of some products they can describe. Then students work in pairs and describe them.

7 If possible, group students from different companies together. Each student thinks of a new product or service that their company is launching or might launch in the near future (or simply invents a product). Give them time to make notes about the product based on the headings. Give help with vocabulary. Students then describe the product or service to the group. You might like to ask the listener to take notes on their partner's descriptions, and then report back to the class.

Pre-work learners
The students either invent a product / service and the details of its development and launch, or recount the history of a product they know. A variation would be for them to research a particular product (e.g. via the Internet) and bring its history and description to a subsequent lesson to tell the class.

ⓘ Refer students to the **Interactive Workbook Glossary** for further study.

Language at work
1 Students look at the photos and match the names to the inventions.

Feedback focus
Do not give the students the correct answers at this point, as this is the focus of the listening in **2**.

2 19▷ Students listen to the radio programme and check their answers.

Answers
1 c **2** d **3** a **4** b

3 20▷ Students read the questions before they listen.

Watch out! You might need to pre-teach *hang up, cell phone, invest*.

Answers
1 electrical engineering
2 Apple
3 Jack Smith
4 Because someone might hear the conversation
5 Because it contained the letters HTML, which is the coding on web pages
6 $300,000
7 July 4th, 1996
8 $400 million

4 Students study the four sentences. You may need to explain some of the grammatical terminology, such as *regular / irregular, negative, infinitive, subject, main verb*.

Answers
a 1 **b** 3 **c** 2 **d** 4

Tip Refer students to the *Tip*, and practise the pronunciation of the four verbs.

Extra activity
Explain the three pronunciations of the *-ed* ending: if the verb ends:
 a in a /t/ or /d/ sound we add /ɪd/ (as stated in the *Tip*)
 b in a voiced sound (i.e. one where you can feel a vibration in your throat) or a vowel, add a /d/ sound
 c in an unvoiced sound (no vibration in the throat), add /t/.

/ɪd/	/d/	/t/

Draw the table on the board. Read out these verbs, and the students write the verbs in the correct column:
arrive check need watch want enjoy invite work walk study serve decide seem wait play close stamp open fill marry die fix hate design launch complete produce like

Answers
/ɪd/: needed, wanted, invited, decided, waited, completed, hated
/d/: arrived, enjoyed, studied, served, seemed, played, closed, opened, filled, married, died, designed, launched
/t/: checked, watched, worked, walked, stamped, fixed, produced, liked

5 Ask students what they know about Tim Berners-Lee. They then read and complete the text.

Watch out! You might like to pre-teach *physics, store, publish, appear, set up, coordinate*.

Answers
1 was born
2 studied
3 built
4 had
5 became
6 spent
7 wrote
8 called
9 didn't publish
10 started
11 appeared
12 set up

» If students need more practice, go to **Practice file 4** on page 109 of the **Student's Book**.

6 Revise who Martin Cooper is (*inventor of the mobile phone*). Stress that the students must not use any of the highlighted words when asking their own questions, as these are the information that their *partner* is looking for. Do not pre-teach anything from the highlighted sections.

Allow weaker students plenty of time to formulate the questions.

Watch out! The first question for both students are passives, so they do not follow the rules in **4**. Teach these separately. Make sure the students include the preposition in end-position where appropriate.

Answers
Student A's questions with answers in brackets:
Where was Martin Cooper born? (Chicago)
What did he study? (electrical engineering)
Who did he start working for? (Motorola)
What was Motorola in a race to make? (the first cell phone)
When was the first public demonstration? (3rd April 1973)
Who did Cooper make the first call to? (Joel Engel)
How much did a smaller version of the phone go on sale for? ($3,500)
What did Cooper become before he set up his own company? (Corporate Director of R+D for Motorola)

Student B's questions with answers in brackets:
When was Martin Cooper born? (1928)
Where did he study? (Illinois Institute of Technology)
What did he help develop? (portable products)
Who was Motorola in a race with? (Bell Laboratories)
Where were the first private tests of the phone? (Washington)
Where did Cooper make the first call by cell phone? (at Bell Laboratories)
When did a smaller version of the phone go on sale? (1983)
What did he call his own company? (Arraycom)

7 Students write down something that is connected to the past, and that will produce sufficient examples of the past simple. Students ask and answer questions as in the example.

Feedback focus

Monitor for correct use of the past simple. You may need to look out for use of subject questions (see notes on exercise 6 in *Language at work* in Unit 3 above) and questions using the verb *be*.

Extra activity

'My last job.'
Students work in pairs to find out as much as possible about their partner's last job. Each student must ask at least eight questions. You could help weaker students by writing prompts on the board.
Pre-work learners can be asked to invent a 'last job'.

Unit 4 | New products

25

Practically speaking

1 21▷ Elicit the importance of showing interest. Students tick the correct phrases. Then play the listening once only for the students to check.

> **Answers**
> The four phrases are:
> Did you?   Was it?
> That's interesting!   Oh really?

2 21▷ The students listen again and complete the extracts.

> **Answers**
> 1 Did you?   3 Was it?
> 2 That's interesting! 4 Oh really?

3 Students practise the dialogues in pairs. Monitor their pronunciation carefully: make sure their intonation is not flat and that they have a good 'up and down' tone.

4 Students follow the instructions and try to keep their conversations going as long as possible.

Business communication

1 Students work in pairs to discuss the questions. Feed back briefly in open class.

> **Answer**
> Podpads are used as outdoor accommodation.

2 22▷ Students think about possible answers to the questions before they listen. Write some of their predictions on the board. Play the listening and ask students to compare their predictions with the audio.

> **Answers**
> 1 To find the most comfortable place for people to stay during outdoor festivals.
> 2 Because they are stronger than tents and can resist rain and wind better. Also, they have an installation team.
> 3 An installation team.
> 4 50
> 5 They offered free accommodation at the festival.
> 6 Twice – once after one night and a second time after a second night.
> 7 They were popular with them, and found the installation teams efficient.
> 8 A success.

Alternative

As an extra practice for past simple questions, ask students to write questions for these answers, all of which are to be found in the text.
1 Last month (*When did the research take place*?)
2 To find the most comfortable place for people to stay during outdoor festivals. (*What was the purpose of the research?*)
3 Because they are stronger than tents and can resist rain and wind better. (*Why did they choose Podpads?*)
4 50 (*How many Podpads did they order?*)
5 Free accommodation (*What did they offer to the 50 visitors?*)
6 After one night and after two nights. (*When did they speak to the visitors?*)
7 They said they were very efficient. (*What did the farmers say about the installation teams?*)

3 22▷ The students match the sentence starts to the endings, then listen to the report again to check their answers.

> **Answers**
> 1 f 2 d 3 b 4 h 5 i 6 g 7 a 8 e 9 c

4 The students put the phrases from **3** in the correct column.

Watch out! Make sure the students know these words from the table: *aim, reason, order, reporting*.

> **Answers**
> Aim of the research: 1, 2
> Reason for doing something: 3
> Order of the process: 4, 5, 7
> Reporting: 6, 8, 9

» If students need more practice, go to **Practice file 4** on page 108 of the **Student's Book.**

5 Ask if it is possible / impossible / recommended in their countries for workers to have a short sleep during the day to increase productivity ('power-napping'). Explain the task.

Divide the class into As and Bs. Each looks at their File. Allow time for students to read their information and prepare their reports, individually, in pairs, or small groups.

Then regroup the students. Each pair gives a report in turn, and together they decide which one is best. Encourage use of the language from **3** and **4** and *Key expressions*.

Watch out! Tell students that the verbs in the Files are in the present, but they will need to change some to the past simple to report on what they did.

Feedback focus
Check the use of report language from **3**. Point out examples of good use of language, and one or two common mistakes, especially in the target language.

One-to-one
Either give a report yourself on one of the Files, after which the student gives theirs, or ask the students to make two reports.

ⓘ Refer students to the **Interactive Workbook Email** and **Phrasebank** sections for further study and to the **Exercises and Tests** for revision.

Case study
Background
This *Case study* presents a situation where a large exhibition site, the Millennium Dome in London, has closed and the various stakeholders need to find a new use for it. It has now opened as the O2 venue. Students then have to give a report on how to develop a similar site in their city.

You might like to ask the students if there are any large sites or venues in their city or country which were built for a particular purpose (e.g. an Expo or an Olympics) and are now unused. What are these sites now used for?

Allow students a few minutes to read the text.

Watch out! Ask the students to guess the meaning of these items: *house* (verb), *access, half that expected*.

Discussion
Students can discuss the questions in pairs before turning to File 09 on page 136 of the Student's Book.

> **Answers**
> 1 The exhibition was disappointing and access by car was difficult.
> 2 Because the Dome was unpopular.
> 3 Students' own answers.

Watch out! You might like to pre-teach *surrounded by, boulevard, leisure attractions, sell-out, forms part of*.

Task
1 Put the students into groups of two or three. Allow students time to read the instructions carefully and decide what to do with the site. Extra ideas can be found in File 09 on page 136 of the Student's Book.

2 Students plan their report using categories in exercise 4 of *Business communication*. Make sure *all* members of each group write down what they are going to say.

3 Regroup the students with one member of the 'company' going to each new group. Each member of the new group gives a report on what they have planned. The others listen as if they were members of the planning department and take notes. At the end, they discuss the plan and vote for the best one.

4 They go back to their original groups and explain which one was chosen and why.

One-to-one
In place of the initial group work, the student and you work together as the company, but the major part of the planning should be done by the student.
Then the student gives the report, and you, as the planning department, give an evaluation of the plan. The student must defend their plan against your criticisms.
Omit part 4 of the Task.

» Unit 4 **Progress test** and **Speaking test**, pages 94–95.

Unit 4 New products

27

5 | Employment

Unit content

By the end of this unit, students will be able to
- talk about job benefits and employment procedures
- describe personal experiences using the present perfect
- delegate work to others
- discuss progress on projects.

Context

Issues surrounding employment and human resources affect everybody, from the benefits on offer to employees, to employer-employee relationships. These can differ enormously from company to company and from country to country. Expectations of the employee can also differ from culture to culture – a French woman working in the USA, for example, may be horrified to learn that she gets only two weeks' holiday a year, and barely three months' maternity leave. In a global, multicultural business environment, employers and employees need to recognize and understand what is expected and acceptable within the culture in which they are working.

This is also the case in less tangible areas, such as the relationships people form with colleagues, bosses, and staff. From the actual recruitment process through to getting on with projects, communicating with team members, allocating tasks, etc., the way people handle their relationships at work is paramount to a successful working environment.

In the first section of this unit, students will focus on the more tangible issues relating to employment, discussing recruitment and employment packages, what is typical in their culture, and what is important to them individually. Later in the unit they look at the issue of delegating and discussing progress. Students are given a range of expressions to help them with these potentially delicate areas, which could otherwise risk offending or being perceived as overbearing. To conclude the unit, the *Case study* looks at a specific recruitment issue and how it was solved.

Starting point

Give students time to consider their responses to the questions. Students answer the questions in pairs and then feed back to open class.

Working with words

1 Pre-teach *employment procedures*. Use the photos to establish the situation. Before reading, ask students to read the questions and discuss possible answers. Then students read the text and write true or false.

> **Answers**
> 1 True   2 True   3 False   4 True

Watch out! Vocabulary from the text that you may wish to pre-teach: *cover* (as a verb), *preferences, choose, vouchers, a waste of money*.

2 Students match the words to make phrases. Allow the use of a dictionary if they are struggling. Don't feed back on the answers, as they are in the listening activity in **3**.

3 23▷ Students listen and check their answers.

> **Answers**
> 1 e   2 f   3 d   4 b   5 c   6 a   7 j   8 g   9 i   10 h

4 23▷ Play the listening again. Students answer the question.

> **Answers**
> **Anna:** useful: flexible hours, paid holiday, private healthcare. Not useful: maternity leave
> **Mark:** useful: company car, mobile phone. Not useful: gym membership
> **Valerie:** useful: subsidized childcare, annual bonus. Not useful: pension scheme

Extension

Stronger students could be asked to do extra listening tasks:
- Why do Anne, Mark and Valerie find the benefits useful / not useful?
- What are the benefits that Mark talks about which are not included in **2**? (Answers: cheap petrol, use of the phone for personal calls, kids can use the laptop at weekends)

5 In pairs, students read the sentences and say which benefits are being described.

> **Answers**
> 1 flexible hours   3 annual bonus
> 2 mobile phone   4 maternity leave

Tip Ask students to read the *Tip* after **5**.

Dictionary activity

Ask the students to read the six sentences and use a good monolingual dictionary to find the meanings of *get*.
1 I get to work at 8.30.
2 Can you get Julie at the airport?
3 We get an annual bonus.
4 I'm sorry. I don't get you.
5 Let's stop. I'm getting tired.
6 I usually get the 6.30 flight.
Answers
1 arrive   2 go and meet   3 receive
4 understand   5 become   6 catch / take

6 Students take turns to describe and guess. Tell them they are not allowed to use the words in the phrases in their descriptions.

Alternative

In pairs: Student A says the first word of the phrase, and Student B completes it and says what it means.

7 Students discuss the benefits in pairs. Stronger students could be asked to negotiate together to come up with the same list. Discuss the different lists in open class to practise the vocabulary further.

One-to-one

Make sure the student doesn't just make a list of six items, but also discusses the reasons for their choice. This will aid retention of the items.

8 Students decide if each thing is done by a candidate or employer. You may need to help with vocabulary, especially *candidate, shortlisted, updates, referees, applies for, fills in, looks through*.

> **Answers**
> candidate: 1, 3, 4, 6, 8   employer: 2, 5, 7, 9

9 Revise the sequencing words like *then* and *after that*. Point out we cannot use *after* as a sequencer. Students put the stages in order.

> **Answers**
> The correct order is 7 – 4 – 8 – 6 – 9 – 1 – 3 – 5 – 2.

>> If students need more practice, go to **Practice file 5** on page 110 of the **Student's Book**.

10 Students discuss in pairs how they got their current job. Pre-teach *accepted*.

Pre-work learners

Students could invent a job that they would like, or talk about a person they know (e.g. a friend, a relative) who has a job.

ⓘ Refer students to the **Interactive Workbook Glossary** for further study.

Language at work

1 24▷ Ask students: *What is a CV? What is the format of a 'normal' CV? What headings would you expect to find on one? What do you think 'a new type of CV' might mean*? Play the conversation and ask students to answer the questions.

> **Answers**
> 1 It's a video CV.   2 Students' own answers

2 24▷ Students listen again and underline the correct verb forms.

> **Answers**
> 1 Have you ever seen   4 have already started
> 2 've never seen   5 has emailed
> 3 read   6 haven't watched

3 Check the names of the two tenses. Students look at the sentences in **2** and say which tense is being used in each. They then complete the rules.

> **Answers**
> All the sentences in **2** use the present perfect except 3, which uses the past simple.
> 1 present perfect   3 has / have
> 2 past simple   4 never, already, yet

4 Point out that time expressions which 'include' the present (including *ever, never, already, yet*) will take the present perfect, and those where the time is finished will take the past simple. Students decide which tense is appropriate for each sentence. Individually, students write sentences using the time expressions. Monitor the use of tenses.

> **Answers**
> 1 present perfect   5 past simple
> 2 past simple   6 present perfect
> 3 past simple   7 present perfect
> 4 present perfect

Unit 5 | Employment

29

5 Students work in pairs. They read out the sentences without the time expression, and their partners guess the expression.

Feedback focus

Make sure students contract *has / have* when they are speaking.

Extra activity

Students write four sentences with different time expressions from **4**. Three sentences must be true, and one false. They read out the sentences to the class, and the other students must guess which one is false.

6 25▷ Direct students' attention to the photo. Ask: *Who is she? Can you tell what kind of job she might be applying for?* Students listen to the extract and say where Naomi has worked.

> **Answers**
> Tanzania

7 25▷ Students use the prompts to make questions. Then they listen again (twice if necessary) and check their answers. For a strong class, **7** and **8** can be combined.

> **Answers**
> 1 When did you start working in the non-profit sector?
> 2 Have you ever worked for a big organization?
> 3 Have you been to Africa in the last year?
> 4 What did you do there?
> 5 And were you happy with the results?

Pronunciation

Make sure students pronounce *have* with the weak form /həv/.

8 25▷ Students listen again and write Naomi's answers.

> **Answers**
> 1 When I left university in 1998.
> 2 No, I haven't.
> 3 Yes, I have.
> 4 My job was to supervise the building of a new school.
> 5 Yes, I was.

» If students need more practice, go to **Practice file 5** on page 111 of the **Student's Book**.

9 Students work in pairs. Point out that while the initial question about their experiences is in the present perfect (often with *ever*), the follow-up questions, which focus on the event itself, are in the past simple. This is a very common pattern in English.

Pre-work learners

You will need to change some of the questions to fit in with your students' context. Some extra questions you could add:
> *Have you ever spoken English outside your school / college?*
> *Have you ever been on holiday with your friends?*
> *Have you ever worked without pay?* (e.g. voluntary or charity work)
> *Have you ever bought anything online?*

Try to elicit a mixture of verbs.

Feedback focus

Monitor for correct use of the tenses and correct pronunciation of *have*.

10 The answers to these questions are, to some extent, subjective and / or dependent on the culture in which they are asked. For example, some people believe it is perfectly acceptable to ask a job applicant their age, whereas in some countries this is considered unacceptable or even illegal. Elicit that the answers to the questions should show the applicant in the best possible light! Make sure there is time to discuss the students' answers in open class.

11 In pairs, students ask and answer three of the questions. Monitor the correct use of present perfect, especially in questions 5, 6, and 8.

Pre-work learners

Give each learner a current job (these could be very different from their projected careers, and include a range of jobs like *postman, bus driver, office worker, judge, teacher*) and ask them to think of extra details to answer questions 2, 5, 6, and 8. They may need more time to prepare for this activity than learners who are in work.

Practically speaking

Start by asking what the verb *delegate* means and why delegation is important. If your learners are managers, ask how much and when they delegate.

1 26▷ Students listen and complete the sentences.

> **Answers**
> 1 need you to
> 2 Please include
> 3 like you to
> 4 Can you
> 5 Could I ask you

2 The students should think about the difficulty of the request and the forms of the verb.

> **Answers**
> 5 is less direct (she uses *could*). She uses it because the request is more difficult.

3 26▷ Students listen again, and match the responses to the questions. They write down Antonio's follow-up information on c and e.

> **Answers**
> 1 b   2 e   3 d   4 a   5 c
> Antonio gives a reason for his refusals: e – he doesn't have the numbers; c – he's got to catch a train.

4 The students in each pair should choose a different box. Students read the boxes, and decide which phrases from **1** would be most appropriate for each request. Students take turns at delegating the work.

Business communication

1 27▷ Students read the instructions. Check they understand the roles of the people involved and the topic of discussion. Students read the notes. Check the meaning of *availability* and *job description*. Students listen to the conversation and complete the notes.

> **Answers**
> 1 next week
> 2 this weekend
> 3 at the end of the month
> 4 Monday morning
> 5 this afternoon
> 6 this afternoon

2 27▷ Students listen a second time and match the sentence beginnings and ends. Give weaker students more time to study the sentences before they listen.

> **Answers**
> 1 f   2 d   3 h   4 g   5 a   6 c   7 e   8 b

Pronunciation

Ask students to listen to the sentences and mark the stressed words. They practise saying the sentences with the correct stress.
Answers
1 Where <u>are</u> we with re<u>cruit</u>ment?
2 We've already <u>short</u>listed <u>twen</u>ty candidates.
3 I <u>e</u>mailed them to you last <u>week</u>.
4 I've been very short of <u>time</u> this week.
5 Time's running <u>out</u>.
6 Leave it to <u>me</u>.
7 I haven't heard what <u>date</u> yet.
8 Have you finished the <u>job</u> description yet?
9 Can you <u>deal</u> with the <u>sala</u>ry issue?

3 Ask students to find equivalent phrases in the nine sentences.

> **Answers**
> a Where are we with …? / Have you … yet?
> b We've already … / I haven't … yet.
> c Leave it with me.
> d Can you deal with …?
> e Time's running out.

4 Check the students understand the new date. Ask them to read through the notes. In pairs, they practise the conversation using the notes. Encourage them to use as many of the phrases in **2** and **3** as they can.

> **Possible answer**
> **Natasha** Where are we with the CVs? Have you read them yet?
> **Ben** Yes, I read them at the weekend. They're all good candidates.
> **Natasha** And have you spoken to the MD about the salaries issue?
> **Ben** No, I haven't, not yet. I didn't have time at the meeting last Friday.
> **Natasha** Well, can you do that this morning? Time's running out.
> **Ben** Yes, OK. For the interviews next week, have we arranged the dates yet?
> **Natasha** No, we haven't. I need to know your availability.
> **Ben** I'm sorry, I've been really busy. I'll confirm by midday. Leave it with me. Have you prepared the job description?
> **Natasha** Yes, I have. I did that over the weekend.

» If students need more practice, go to **Practice file 5** on page 110 of the **Student's Book**.

Unit 5 | Employment

31

5 Teach the phrase *to-do list*. Ask the students if they keep one. Explain they are going to make a to-do list for this month at their work. Students read the *Key expressions* – check they can pronounce them with good stress and intonation. They then exchange papers, ask each other about progress with the tasks, and, if necessary, delegate the tasks to their partner.

Watch out! Students should note that when they say when they did a task, the tense will usually be past simple. Make sure they use the adverbs *already* and *yet* correctly: *already* is used with affirmative sentences and goes between the auxiliary verb *has / have* and the main verb, whereas *yet* is used with negatives and questions and goes at the end.

Pre-work learners

Students imagine they are in a job, and invent appropriate tasks for that job. A variation would be for you to ask them to imagine they are a famous entrepreneur (e.g. Bill Gates) and make a list for them.

One-to-one

Both you and the student should make to-do lists, so that the student gets a chance to use the questions, and react to the delegation language.

Refer students to the **Interactive Workbook Email** and **Phrasebank** sections for further study and to the **Exercises and Tests** for revision.

Case study

Background

This *Case study* focuses on an international NGO (Oxfam) which has had problems with its recruitment processes, and as a result, has turned to an online solution. This is expected to be cheaper, reach more people geographically (partly because it is online, partly because it can be in different languages), and be more flexible, because failed or interested applications can still be kept for future use.

The *Task* is in two parts: the first involves the students discussing the progress made with improving HR systems so far (thus practising the language of the unit). In the second, the students decide on what the organization should do next.

As a lead-in, ask the students what an NGO is, and if they can name any others, e.g. UNICEF. Ask: *what considerations might a company or organization have when recruiting staff?* These might be:

- how to get the best staff
- where to advertise jobs – the cost v the effectiveness of different places
- timescale: when to recruit and how long the process should take
- how to interview applicants – face to face? focus groups? problem-solving tasks?

Discussion

Students then read the text entitled *Recruiting talent fast* and discuss the questions in open class or in small groups. Once they have had plenty of time to discuss, ask them to read File 11 on page 137 of the Student's Book.

Watch out! In order for students to understand the text in detail, you may need to pre-teach *NGO, humanitarian crises, fundraising, diverse workforce, equal opportunities, web-based e-recruitment solution*.

> **Answers**
> 1 It can't pay very high salaries, so it finds it difficult to recruit top-quality professionals.
> 2 It can't spend much money on recruitment but it has to have a diverse workforce and equal opportunities.
> 3 Students' own answers

Watch out! Possibly problematic vocabulary items in File 11: *monitored, stored, talent bank, abroad*.

Task

1 Students read the Files carefully.
2 Students work in pairs. They discuss the problems from six months ago, and the progress made. Encourage use of the language in the unit.

Students could either stay in pairs, or form new groups of four. They discuss whether the organization should adopt a web-based solution as Oxfam did. If they decide not to, they should come up with three concrete ideas for improving the recruitment and retention still further, but without spending too much money.

Finally, the whole class should discuss the issue and feed back on what they decided.

One-to-one

A variation could be to give both Files to the student, and ask him / her to play the role of the organization's HR manager, with you as the director. You question the student about progress made and suggestions for the future.

» Unit 5 **Progress test** and **Speaking test**, pages 96–97.

6 | Customer service

Unit content

By the end of this unit, students will be able to
- talk about customer service rules and experiences
- make comparisons
- respond to complaints
- ask for and give opinions.

Context

Customer service is a field which has become of increasing importance over recent years, as companies try to find the added value that will attract and, as importantly, retain customers. This field has even become a separate area of business expertise, with various 'gurus' being hired by companies to improve their performance.

One part of customer service which is particularly vital is that of dealing with complaints. No company can avoid things occasionally going wrong, but the way in which it copes with that situation can make a strong positive – or negative – impression on the customer. In this way, complaints become an opportunity as well as a problem.

Finding out the opinions of customers is a key way to maintain or improve customer service. Many business people believe the modern company should canvass the opinions of members of staff as well as customers on important issues.

This unit focuses on customer service from two points of view: as workers (or potential workers) in companies that deal with customers, and as customers themselves. Students will learn how to talk about customer service rules and experiences. They will also learn about making comparisons and responding to complaints. The unit also gives help and practice in the area of asking for and giving opinions, then wraps up with some real world examples of customer service in the *Case study*.

Starting point

Students can discuss the questions as a class. For question 1, ask them if they have any recent experience of contacting a company, and what happened. For 2, you could ask them to formulate 'rules' for good customer service, starting with 'Always …' and 'Never …'

Working with words

1 You could ask them to read the rules first, as this follows on closely from the previous discussion. Use the photo to set the scene. They then discuss how many of the rules are followed by their company.

2 Students match the quotes to the rules.

Answers
a 5 b 6 c 4 d 3 e 2 f 1

3 Students match the expressions in bold to the definitions. To reinforce the phrases, ask students to suggest other ways in which companies could do these things.

Answers
1 encourage customer loyalty
2 offer a personalized service
3 conduct surveys
4 meet the needs of the customers
5 keep to your delivery dates
6 deal with complaints
7 get repeat business

Watch out! Check the stress on the verb *conduct*: con*duct*.

4 Students should complete the sentences without looking back at 3. They then discuss the questions in pairs.

Answers
1 meet 2 keep 3 conduct 4 deal 5 offer 6 encourage

Pre-work learners

Students could talk about a company that they know as a customer.

5 28▷ Ask students if they have had any experience of poor customer service. Ask what happened and what the effect was on them. Play the listening and students complete the table.

Answers
1 Book was in the wrong language. Shop did not have the correct version and refused to give a refund.
2 Taxi was late and speaker missed their flight.
3 A new chair broke in the first week. Customer had to phone nine times in two months to get a new chair.

33

6 28▷ Students complete the sentences with the words in the list. They then listen again and check.

> **Answers**
> 1 impossible
> 2 helpful
> 3 unreliable
> 4 loyal
> 5 dissatisfied

Feedback focus / Pronunciation
Make sure they say the words with the correct stress.
dis*sat*isfied, *help*ful, im*poss*ible, *loy*al, unre*li*able

Tip Draw the students' attention to the *Tip*. You could ask them to suggest other words with these prefixes. Note that *im-* becomes *in-* or *il-* depending on the first letter of the adjective.

Extra activity
Ask students to find the opposites of these adjectives in a good dictionary.
likely, legal, loyal, helpful, agreeable, probable, wanted, economical, intelligent, happy, correct, patient, friendly, polite, employed, honest

7 Student A explains a word from **6**, and B must say it. For stronger students, a variation could be that A gives an example of the word, and B must say it.

Dictionary activity
Ask students to choose six long words from this section (i.e. more than two syllables). (The words in **5** would be particularly good.) They use a good monolingual dictionary to find the stressed syllable in each word. Ask: *How does your dictionary show the stress? If there are two stresses in a word, how does it show the primary and secondary stress?*

» If students need more practice, go to **Practice file 6** on page 112 of the **Student's Book.**

8 Weaker students could make notes for each prompt. Students who cannot think of examples from their own experience should invent! You may need to feed in vocabulary, especially for part 5 (possible vocabulary: *angry, irritated, frustrated, impatient, surprised*). Students work in pairs and tell each other about their experiences.

Watch out! You may need to teach *after-sales support service* and *repeat business*.

ⓘ Refer students to the **Interactive Workbook Glossary** for further study.

Language at work

1 Students discuss the questions in pairs. Make sure you also take time to discuss them in open class. NB you will get a wide range of responses to these questions. Students who never shop online should talk about their friends' or colleagues' experiences.

2 29▷ Students listen to the extract and compare their answers.

> **Answers**
> The quickest way is by telephone.

3 29▷ Students listen again and underline the correct word. Tell the students that the wording in the listening is not the same as in the exercise.

> **Answers**
> 1 less difficult
> 2 The cheapest
> 3 better
> 4 isn't

4 You may need to explain *comparative* and *superlative* (Key: we use the comparative when we are comparing two things; superlative for three or more.) Ask students to complete the rules using the adjectives in **3**.

> **Answers**
> 1 the cheapest
> 2 more difficult
> 3 better / worse
> 4 as … as …

Watch out! Two more useful rules that you might want to add:
- one-syllable adjectives that end in *-ed* are an exception to rule 1: they take *more* and *the most* (e.g. *more tired, more bored*)
- *less* and *the least* are not used with short adjectives: we use *not as … instead* (*not as good, not as fast*).

Tip Students read the *Tip*, which relates to two-syllable adjectives.

Extension
Give students sentence beginnings with an adjective and ask students to complete them with a comparative or superlative, e.g.
Texaco is a big company, but Shell … (is bigger / is the biggest oil company in the world)
Bill Gates is intelligent, but Einstein … (was more intelligent / was the most intelligent man who has ever lived)
You can do this orally or in writing.

5 30▷ Students can be encouraged to predict the answers to the questions, so give them a few minutes to discuss possible answers. They then listen and confirm (or not) their predictions.

> **Answers**
> 1 the 16–24 age group / men
> 2 searching for information about goods and services, and sending and receiving emails
> 3 from home
> 4 because we don't have time
> 5 films and music

Extra activity
If your students need to understand and say figures, copy the audio script on page 151, and white out the statistics in the text. Students listen again and fill them in.

6 30▷ The students complete the results in the sentences 1–6. They then listen again to check. Explain to the students that this is not a gap-filling exercise: they have to interpret the information in the extract in order to check they have completed the sentences correctly.

> **Answers**
> 1 the lowest   4 more common
> 2 as popular   5 The most important
> 3 more interested   6 as high

» If students need more practice, go to **Practice file 6** on page 113 of the **Student's Book**.

7 Check the vocabulary in the table. Students work in pairs. You may like to pair weaker with stronger students for this activity. Stronger students could be asked to do this activity orally.

Alternative
Organize this activity as a role-play. Students (in groups of three) must decide where and how to buy all the items in column 1. Encourage use of the comparatives and superlatives, e.g.
  A *Let's buy the flowers online. It's cheaper than in the shops.*
  B *But the staff in a shop are more helpful. Shops are much better for things like flowers.*

Practically speaking

1 31▷ Start by asking students when was the last time they complained about something. Teach the phrase *make a complaint (+ about)*. Check the students understand the situations a–c. Students listen and number the complaints.

> **Answers**
> a 2   b 3   c 1

2 31▷ Students listen again and match the response to the complaint in **1**.

> **Answers**
> 1 b (Call 3)   2 c (Call 1)   3 a (Call 2)

3 31▷ Students listen a third time, and complete the apologies.

> **Answers**
> 1 I'm very sorry about that.
> 2 It's our mistake. I'm terribly sorry.
> 3 I do apologize for that.

Pronunciation
Ask students to mark the stress (which is particularly important here) and imitate the intonation of the complaints and responses:
That <u>is</u> a <u>prob</u>lem.
I <u>see</u>.
Oh <u>right</u>.
I'm <u>very</u> sorry about <u>that</u>.
It's <u>our</u> mistake. I'm <u>terri</u>bly sorry.
I <u>do</u> apologize for <u>that</u>.

4 Give students a minute to read the situations and rehearse their conversations. Then, in pairs, they practise the complain–respond–apologize routines.

Business communication

1 32▷ Students listen to the managers talking and answer the questions.

> **Answers**
> 1 that the staff are rude, and don't know anything about their products; the refunds policy is too strict
> 2 to give sales staff a week's training before they start; to exchange the product if there is no receipt

Unit 6 | Customer service

35

Watch out! You may need to pre-teach / revise some of the vocabulary in the conference call: *rude, polite, profile, deal with (customers), refunds policy, strict, purchase, expense, receipt*. NB the 'p' in *receipt* is silent.

2 32▷ Play the conversation again and ask students to write down phrases they hear with the three verbs.

> **Answers**
> **think:** I think … / I think you're right. / What do you think? / I don't think …
> **agree:** I don't agree. / I agree with you. / I don't agree at all. / Do you agree?
> **feel:** I don't feel … / How do you feel about that? / Personally, I feel …

3 Students write the expressions in the correct section.

> **Answers**
> **ask for an opinion:** What do you think? / Do you agree? / How do you feel about that?
> **give an opinion:** I think … / I don't think … / I don't feel … / Personally, I feel …
> **agree:** I think you're right. / I agree with you.
> **disagree:** I don't agree. / I don't agree at all.

Pronunciation

Make sure the students say the phrases with acceptable stress and intonation. Agreeing and disagreeing is a potentially sensitive area, and for some students it is acceptable in their own language or culture to disagree more forcefully than would be the case in English. Use the recording of the conference call discussion to provide a model, or say the phrases yourself and ask students to repeat.

4 Give the students a few minutes to read the ideas. Check they understand the vocabulary. Weaker students could write a few notes to help them in the discussion. Then in pairs or small groups, students give their opinions about the ideas. Encourage them to use the phrases in **3** as much as possible. (See alternative below.)

Alternative

To ensure students use the phrases, copy them out onto individual cards. Each pair or group has the cards on the table in front of them, and each time they use one of the phrases, they take the card. At the end, the winner is the one with the most cards.

» If students need more practice, go to **Practice file 6** on page 112 of the **Student's Book**.

5 Explain the context carefully. Teach the word *proposals*. Ask the students to read the proposals, and check the vocabulary. The students discuss the proposals as a group and decide on one option. Encourage them to use the phrases from **3** and the *Key expressions*.

Feedback focus

Watch out for the stress and intonation that students use, especially when disagreeing. Make sure they say *I don't think …* + affirmative (rather than *I think …* + negative).

ⓘ Refer students to the **Interactive Workbook Email** and **Phrasebank** sections for further study and to the **Exercises and Tests** for revision.

Case study

Background

This *Case study* is slightly different from the others so far in this book, as the students do not work as staff of a company, but as judges deciding which company should receive an award, in this case for customer service. The basic premise, that of the National Customer Services Awards, is authentic, though of course the companies presented here are invented.

The importance of customer service should be clear to the students, both from their own experience and from the work so far in this unit. In the first part, the students read about different ways in which a company has impressed or surprised a customer with the level or type of their service. In the second, they must decide together which of the companies deserves to be given the award. This allows them to use the agreeing, disagreeing, and opinion language from the unit.

As a lead-in, ask the students to think of surprising or innovative ways that a company could provide good service to their customers. Stress the WOW factor – something that makes a customer sit up and take notice! Then ask students to move on to the text.

Extra activity

Set the students these questions to check their understanding of the text.
1 What does Derek Williams believe?
2 What is the role of price competition and product promotion?
3 What is the WOW factor?

Suggested answers
1 Companies should make customers fall in love with them.
2 Important but not as important as employees and existing customers.
3 The ability of the company to surprise or impress its customers.

Discussion

Questions 1–3 can be discussed in open class, or in small groups. For question 4, students read File 14 on page 138 of the Student's Book.

> **Answers**
> 1 They can use the award to promote their business.
> 2 The categories include teams, individuals, and innovation.
> 3 Students' own answers

Task

1 Students work in groups of four. Each student in the group reads about a different company in File 13. For smaller groups, students could be asked to read about two or more companies (and see Alternative below).

2 The students come together and each one presents the story of their company. Encourage them to do this in their own words, and / or from memory, and not just read aloud. For the discussion that follows, remind the students to use the opinion language from the unit. You could stipulate that they must argue their own company's case, but are not allowed to vote for it at the end. At the end, each group decides which company should be given the award.

Alternative

If your class does not lend itself to groups of four, ask the students simply to read through the four reports about the companies. As they are reading, they should mentally rank the companies in terms of the WOW factor. This will prepare them for the discussion that follows.

One-to-one

Your student reads the four reports, and he / she and you discuss them together. If you want the student to do the reporting phase, ask him / her to read just two or three reports and summarize them. You take the others.

Extra activity

Students write a report for the Awards website
- describing which company won the award, and why
- mentioning two other deserving companies.

» Unit 6 **Progress test** and **Speaking test**, pages 98–99.

7 | Travel

Unit content

By the end of this unit, students will be able to
- use vocabulary about hotels and airports
- ask for travel information using countable and uncountable nouns
- report to a company reception
- make small talk and develop a conversation.

Context

Travel is important to many business people – in the past it was only the top executives that travelled for work, but nowadays in this global community, people at any level of an organization may find themselves being asked to travel abroad for a conference, a training session, a meeting, etc. And travelling is not just about the process of getting to your destination. Once there, the business person needs to be able to converse with their host. This requires a certain amount of skill in small talk and social English.

Attitudes to small talk and socializing vary from one culture to another. In certain European countries, for example, the use of small talk to facilitate business encounters is regarded as unnecessary, while in the Middle East and many other places, it would be unthinkable to launch into a business meeting without the requisite time spent on non-business subjects.

Furthermore, socializing is often an area where non-native speakers feel least comfortable. Whereas they can often talk about the technical aspects of their work with fluency, they are much less confident about discussing matters like family and interests. Of course, you don't do business with somebody on the quality of their small talk, but socializing undoubtedly plays a vital part in the building up of business contacts. A study by an American university found that 80% of the time, it is lack of communication skills that hold people back in their careers, rather than technical know-how or ability.

In this unit, students will learn to talk about travel, with a focus on countable and uncountable nouns. They will also practise reporting to a company reception as well as making small talk. The unit ends with a game where they can put what they have learnt in the unit into practice.

Starting point

You could ask the students to discuss the questions in pairs and small groups.

Watch out! Watch out for correct use of prepositions: *on foot* but *by car / train / plane*.

Pre-work learners

Ask students to answer the questions for their school / college or for a holiday / weekend job they have done.

Working with words

1 Ask students if they have heard of or used Yotels. If so, get them to explain what they are and how they are different from normal hotels. If not, ask them to look at the photo and suggest answers to the questions. They then read the text and answer the questions.

Watch out! Possible vocabulary in the text for pre-teaching / revising: *chain (of hotels), catch up on, check in, techno wall, shuttle bus, waste time*.

> **Answers**
> 1 Guests stay in cabins, not rooms. They can stay for just four hours. They don't have to make a reservation. Check-in is via a machine.
> 2 If they have a delay, an early flight, or a long wait between connections.
> 3 Techno wall with TV, the Internet, bed / sofa, shower rooms
> 4 Guests don't have to take a shuttle bus to the terminal.

2 Students discuss the questions in pairs.

> **Suggested answers**
> **the location:** Yotels are conveniently situated for airport departures, saving time
> **the facilities:** the rooms have most things that a business traveller would need
> **the time:** business people can avoid wasting time when delayed or in transit; they can use the delay to catch up on work, etc.

3 33▷ Students look at the three texts and say where they would see them. They then listen and complete the texts.

> **Answers**
> 1 delayed
> 2 departure lounge
> 3 boarding
> 4 Gate
> 5 check out
> 6 key card
> 7 safe
> 8 bill
> 9 flight
> 10 one-way
> 11 lands
> 12 terminal

4 Students look at the words in bold in **1** and the words they have written in **3** and write them in the table.

> **Answers**
> **Hotels:** reservation, check-in, key card, facilities, double, single, luggage, safe, check out, bill, leave
> **Airports:** terminals, delayed, connections, shuttle bus, check-in desk, departure lounge, boarding, gate, flight, one-way, lands

Tip Refer students to the *Tip* about *travel, trip,* and *journey*.

» If students need more practice, go to **Practice file 7** on page 114 of the **Student's Book.**

5 Divide the class into pairs. As read File 15 on page 138 of the Student's Book. Bs look at File 40 on page 143. Give the students a few minutes to prepare and rehearse. Weaker students could make notes.

6 You could use this activity as a chance to revise the past simple from Unit 4, including the pronunciation of *-ed* endings and irregular past simple forms. To make the activity more interactive, you could ask the listeners to take notes and report to the class.

Pre-work learners
Students could invent a business trip.

Extra activity
If your students need more practice with past simple questions, change **6** to a conversation where one student can only ask Yes / No questions about Student A's trip, e.g:
Did you go to the USA?
Did you go on business or for a holiday?
Did you stay in a nice hotel?

ⓘ Refer students to the **Interactive Workbook Glossary** for further study.

Language at work

1 Students read the questions in pairs. As they are reading, monitor for problems with vocabulary. Students then discuss the answers either for the airport nearest to where they are now, or to where they live / work. Students could pretend to be the information officer of their local airport.

2 34▷ Use the photo to set the scene. Ask if any students have been to Narita. Students who use the airport regularly could be asked the questions in **1**. Explain that they are going to listen to a representative from the airport giving information. Students decide which question from **1** is not answered. Explain that they do not need to answer the questions at this point.

Watch out! You may wish to pre-teach the following.
option = choice
fares = the money you pay for a ticket on transport
towels = cloths to dry your hands
hairdryers = machines for drying your hair

> **Answers**
> Question 2 is not answered.

3 34▷ Students listen again and write notes. Explain that they only need to listen for the necessary information – they do not need to understand every word.

> **Answers**
> 1 Yes, there are two train services. Taxis cost from 14,000 yen.
> 3 Five
> 4 In the Check-in area of Departures
> 5 Yes, in both terminals.
> 6 Yes, you can.

4 You could start this section by writing two lists of types of food on the board, one containing countable items like *bananas, apples, biscuits* and the other uncountable items like *milk, sugar, soup*. Students say what each list has in common. Students complete the rules.

> **Answers**
> 1 Countable
> 2 Uncountable
> 3 countable, uncountable
> 4 countable, uncountable, countable

5 Students read the FAQs in **1** again, and identify the countable and uncountable nouns.

> **Answers**
> **Countable:** airport, taxi, terminals, shuttle bus, meeting, shower rooms, cash machines, suitcase, lockers, phone, trip
> **Uncountable:** public transport, time, money, luggage

Tip Refer students to the *Tip* about nouns that can be countable and uncountable. Ask them if they can think of any other examples.

Dictionary activity
Stronger students could be asked to use a good monolingual dictionary to find the meanings and examples for the following words which can be both countable and uncountable: *glass, work, land, paper, stone, coffee, cheese, chocolate, wood, light*.

Unit 7 | Travel

39

6 Students label the nouns countable or uncountable. They could say if this is the same or different in their language.

Watch out! Students may point out that *work* can be countable with a different meaning (e.g. *roadworks, works of art*). *News* looks like a plural, but is singular (we say *The news is bad*).

> **Answers**
> taxi C night C bank C research U equipment U minute C
> product C hour C business trip C travel U job C work U
> news U information U

7 Students complete the questions with a suitable phrase, and then ask and answer the questions in pairs. If the students work in the same office, change *office* to *home* in questions **1** and **6**.

> **Answers**
> 1 Is there   4 Are there
> 2 How much   5 How much
> 3 How many   6 Is there

Pre-work learners
Change *office* to *home* in questions 1 and 6; change *business trips* to *trips abroad* in question 3; change question 4 to *… many students from overseas in your school?*

» If students need more practice, go to **Practice file 7** on page 115 of the **Student's Book**.

8 The Files for this exercise are quite detailed, so give the students plenty of time to read them and absorb the information. In particular, the students who will be asking the questions need time to formulate them, either in their heads or (for weaker students) in writing. Encourage students to use the question language from **7**.

Feedback focus
Monitor for correct use of countable and uncountable nouns, and the question forms from **7**. Make a note of common mistakes, and bring them to the students' attention at the end: you could write them on the board and ask students to correct themselves.

Practically speaking

1 35▷ Briefly set the scene. Students listen to the first conversation and decide if he is polite. In pairs, they discuss how he could be more polite. Allow the students to discuss the answers in open class too. NB you will need to pause the recording after Conversation 1 ready for Exercise 2.

> **Suggested answers**
> No, he isn't polite.
> He doesn't say *Hello*.
> He uses *I want* instead of *I'd like to*.
> He gives very short answers.

2 35▷ The students listen to the second conversation and order the information.

> **Answers**
> 1 d   2 a   3 c   4 b

3 35▷ Students listen to the second conversation again. They decide who is speaking, and complete the sentences.

Watch out! Check students understand the difference between *sign* and *sign in*.

> **Answers**
> 1 C My name's Helen Edwards and **I'm from** Citibank.
> 2 C I have **an appointment** with Susana Kechel at 11 o'clock.
> 3 R Would you like to take **a seat** while you're waiting?
> 4 C Do I need to **sign in**?
> 5 R Here's your **security pass**.

4 In pairs, students practise the conversation first as themselves, for which they will need to invent the name of their company and the person they are visiting, and then using the prompts. You could re-arrange the classroom furniture to make it seem more like a real company reception, with the customers entering the classroom, and receptionists sat behind a desk.

Business communication

1 Pre-teach the phrase *small talk*. Ask the students to discuss the question. NB if you have a mixed nationality class, you may find students disagree about the usefulness of small talk: in some cultures, it is considered a waste of time, whereas in others, it is an essential part of the business meeting process. How long the small talk goes on, and what you talk about, also depends on how well you know the person you are meeting.

2 36▷ Students listen to the conversation and decide which topics from **1** are being discussed. Play the conversation once only.

Watch out! Since this activity practises listening for the topic of a conversation (a very useful skill in a foreign language), you may not wish to pre-teach vocabulary.

> **Answers**
> Topics discussed are: the journey, holidays, interests. (Dan mentions his wife, but they don't really talk about family.)

3 36▷ Students listen again and complete the questions.

> **Answers**
> 1 Did 4 did
> 2 Do 5 Are
> 3 Did 6 do

4 Students complete the table with the expressions from **3**. After checking the answers, spend some time on the meaning and pronunciation of the other sentences too.

> **Answers**
> Asking about a journey: *Did you have a good flight?*
> Asking about experiences: *Did you see the Alhambra?*
> Asking about habits: *Do you often travel abroad on business? When do you usually take your holiday?*
> Asking about opinions / interests: *What did you think of it? Are you interested in architecture?*

Pronunciation

Showing interest through your intonation is particularly important here. Ask students to repeat the sentences after you paying attention to stress and intonation.

» If students need more practice, go to **Practice file 7** on page 114 of the **Student's Book**.

5 Students work in pairs, and make questions about the topics in **1**. Weaker students should be encouraged to keep closely to the form of the questions in **4**. Make sure both students write all the questions.

> **Possible answers**
> **Your job**
> What time do you usually start work?
> How often do you have to attend meetings?
> Do you usually leave work on time?
> Do you often go away on business?
> How do you get on with your team?
> Do you have your own office?

Your journey
How was the flight?
Have you been here before?
How did you get to the airport?
Was the plane full?

Your country
What time do people get up in your country?
What do people usually have for lunch?
How do people usually spend their free time?
How often do people go out for dinner?
Do people ever walk to work?
Where do people usually go on holiday?

Your family
Have you got any children?
Are you married?
Do you live near your family?
How often do you see your family?
Do you spend a lot of time together?
Have you got any brothers and sisters?

Your interests
What type of (books) do you (read)?
Do you like …?
Have you ever been (diving)?
Do you enjoy (going to concerts)?
What do you like doing …?

Your holidays
Have you been away this year?
When was your last holiday?
Where did you go?
Have you ever been to Asia?
How long do you have off in the summer?
Do you prefer the beach or the mountains?

Feedback focus

Focus on correct use and pronunciation of auxiliary verbs, especially *did, do*, and verb *be*. If the students are having problems, refer them to the examples in **4**.

6 Students change partners. They should have twelve questions to ask their new partner.

7 Ask students to study the *Key expressions*. Check for any problems with vocabulary. Then ask them to role-play conversations in pairs, with one student visiting the other's country. If all the students come from the same country, ask them to invent the answers or pretend they are American, etc. As before, make sure they ask questions with the correct intonation (often more important than correct grammar in real-life communication).

Alternative

Prepare sets of four role cards, two for visitors and two for hosts. The cards should include: name, company name, nationality, family, interests, last holiday, and likes and dislikes. Distribute these cards for the role-play. Make sure everybody plays a visitor and a host at some point.

ⓘ Refer students to the **Interactive Workbook Email** and **Phrasebank** sections for further study and to the **Exercises and Tests** for revision.

Activity

Background

The objective of this game is to practise the language for this unit. Each pair will need a coin and a counter or small object each.

Procedure

Ask the students to read the instructions and study the board for a few moments. Check they understand the rules, and the vocabulary. (The rules of the game are such that they will have to visit every square on their side of the board.) Weaker students could be given time to prepare and rehearse the conversations mentally, but don't let them write anything down, as the idea of the game is to produce spontaneous speech.

Alternative

Ask the students to monitor each other's output. If they spot a mistake, the other student must go back a square. If they disagree about the mistake, you should arbitrate.

Feedback focus

Divide the board into two sections. On the left, write down noteworthy examples of sentences and phrases said by the students during the game. (Or do this on an OHP transparency – this distracts the students less.) On the right, write down sentences with mistakes. At the end, draw students' attention to the 'good' sentences, and ask them to correct the mistakes. (A more challenging alternative is to write down all the phrases, and ask students to decide if they are 'good' or 'mistaken'.)

» Unit 7 **Progress test** and **Speaking test**, pages 100–101.

8 | Orders

Unit content

By the end of this unit, students will be able to
- talk about orders and deliveries
- talk about the future using the present continuous, *going to*, and *will*
- make arrangements
- make and respond to suggestions.

Context

Processing orders is one of the areas within the larger remit of Logistics. The success of a company depends very much on the effectiveness of their order and delivery systems. Companies are continuously looking at how to streamline their systems and one direction in which many companies are turning is online retailing. This is an area of retailing which has expanded enormously in recent years, at least in some countries. There are some products and services, such as airline tickets, where the first method of purchase for most customers would be the Internet, which has made the process of buying a ticket simple and relatively painless. For other goods, such as food or clothes, the uptake has been more patchy. Online retailers like Amazon have become leading figures in the retail of books, CDs, and electrical goods. They have developed a fast and cost-effective order and delivery system which benefits both the retailer and the customer.

Increasingly, companies are asking their staff to contribute ideas to make the company more efficient or profitable. Some even give their employees a bonus or a commission for such ideas.

The unit presents relevant language for talking about orders and deliveries, which is also the theme of the *Case study*. Students will also practise talking about the future. The language of making and responding to suggestions is one which is highly relevant to all business people nowadays. This unit presents useful language for this.

Starting point

You could start by asking the students to make a list of all the goods that they have bought online in the last year and from this calculate which goods are the most frequently bought. (According to a recent survey, the top three are computer and electronic goods, office supplies, and clothes and accessories.) Then discuss the questions with the students in open class.

Working with words

1 Start by asking students if they ever use Amazon, and if so, if they have noticed the name of the company which delivers the goods (answer: UPS). Find out what they know about the two companies. Students read the text and answer the questions.

Suggested answers
1 They were both founded in Seattle. They are both the biggest company in their field.
2 That they will deliver the goods quickly, and they will provide choice, competitive prices, and excellent customer service.
3 By allowing Amazon to process orders quickly, and to quote prices for a range of delivery options. By allowing the customers to track the shipment, and to use UPS's returns services.
4 The tools are popular with customers, and Amazon can cut costs.

2 Students match the words from the text to the definitions. Weaker students could use a dictionary.

Watch out! Make sure the students pronounce *purchase* and *enquiry* correctly. In American English, *enquiry* is usually spelt *inquiry* and pronounced with the stress on the first syllable. If students ask you about *invoice,* refer them to the *Tip* below.

Answers
1 g 2 j 3 b 4 f 5 d 6 e 7 h 8 a 9 i 10 c

3 After they have completed the matching, check thoroughly that the students understand the meaning of the phrases. In pairs, they take turns to put the phrases into a sentence.

Answers
1 quote
2 pay
3 place
4 check
5 deliver
6 process
7 track
8 make
9 make
10 deliver

4 37▷ Check students understand *supplier*. Students work in pairs to order the sentences. They then listen and check their answers.

Answers
The correct order is b – e – d – j – h - g – i – a – f – c.

Unit 8 | Orders

43

Tip Refer students to the *Tip* about *invoice* and *bill*.

» If students need more practice, go to **Practice file 8** on page 116 of the **Student's Book**.

5 Students work in pairs and take it in turns to describe a recent ordering experience. If students haven't ordered anything recently, they should invent.

One-to-one

Ask your student to tell their story first. Then, as extra practice of the target language, tell your own story, and get the student to ask questions about what you did next:
You … *but the goods never arrived.*
Student *So did you make a complaint?*

ⓘ Refer students to the **Interactive Workbook Glossary** for further study.

Language at work

1 38▷ Students look at the photo and speculate on how the customer is feeling and why. Students listen and complete the message pad.

> **Answers**
> Client: **Houghton** Consulting
> Order number: **762 / 29 B**
> Original delivery date: **Monday 26th February**
> New delivery date: **Thursday 8th March**
> Action: change delivery date to **Friday 2nd March**

2 Point out that the three sentences all talk about the future, but have different grammatical forms. Refer them to the title of this section if necessary. They complete the rules and examples.

Watch out! Students may have learned that *will* is 'the future tense' in English. You may wish to point out that there are several forms in English for talking about the future, depending on the speaker's point of view, and when the decision was made. *Will* is most commonly used for decisions at the moment of speaking (as here), offers and promises (*I'll call you tomorrow*), and objective predictions. (*I will* is usually contracted to *I'll*.)

> **Answers**
> 1 *will* Example: I'll call you back.
> 2 *going to* Example: We're going to deliver the cards …
> 3 *present continuous* Example: We're attending the company conference …

3 Students should do the matching first, as this gives them clues as to which future form is most likely.

> **Answers**
> 1 d I'm having
> 2 e I'll ask
> 3 f We're going to advertise … (NB it could also be 'We're advertising …', for example, if the speaker has already fixed a date for the advertisement.)
> 4 b I'm meeting (It could also be 'I'm going to meet …')
> 5 a I'll change
> 6 c I'm going to buy

Feedback focus

Make sure students omit *to* with *will* and include it with *going to*. Ask students to justify their answers.

Extension

Ask students to practise the exchanges in pairs with books closed.

4 Stronger students should do this activity without preparation. Students ask and answer the questions in pairs, making sure they choose the correct future form.

Watch out! In numbers 3 and 5, the present continuous is possible, but that would have a present meaning.

> **Answers**
> 1 I'm meeting   6 I'm going
> 2 I'll pick   7 I'm playing
> 3 I'm going to look   8 We're going to book
> 4 I'll give   9 I'll go
> 5 I'm going to look

» If students need more practice, go to **Practice file 8** on page 117 of the **Student's Book**.

5 Students could change partners for this activity. Make sure they don't simply repeat the ideas from **4**!

Feedback focus

Focus on students' use of future forms. Since the correct use of these forms depends on what the speaker is thinking, it is not always possible to say something is correct or incorrect simply from what they say. Write down ambiguous or dubious examples, and discuss them afterwards with the class. Ask concept questions like *Are you deciding now, or have you already decided? Are you talking about now or the future?*

Practically speaking

1 Explain that all the phrases come from the same conversation. Students read and decide if the conversation is formal or informal.

> **Answer**
> Formal

2 39▷ Students listen and say why and when Fenola and the supplier are meeting.

> **Answers**
> They're meeting on Wednesday at 11 to discuss ideas for the new software application.

3 40▷ Students listen to the second conversation and answer the same questions.

> **Answers**
> They're meeting for lunch on Thursday at 12.30.

4 40▷ Students listen again and write equivalent expressions to the ones in **1**. To check their answers, students read the audio script on page 153 of the Student's Book.

> **Answers**
> 1 Can we meet   4 make it
> 2 are you free   5 How about
> 3 Is … for you?   6 Sounds

5 Elicit that the first conversation will use mainly formal language, and the second informal. Encourage students to use the future forms from this unit.

Feedback focus

Focus on the use of the correct register in each conversation, and future forms.

Alternative

Tell the person who is being phoned that they do not want to have the presentation or play tennis, so they should invent reasons and excuses to avoid the appointment. This will mean they have to use more future forms. It also makes the activity more fun.

Business communication

1 Ask the students to work in pairs and talk about their company logos.

Pre-work learners

Take in a few examples of well-known company logos (cars and trainers are good examples) and ask students to say which company it is. Ask them to say which ones work best and why.

2 41▷ Ask why companies change their logo, and if any of the students' companies have changed their logo recently. Play the conversation and students answer the questions.

> **Answers**
> 1 They decide to shorten the name on the logo to RAS.
> 2 They decide to ask a few local designers for samples of their work.

3 41▷ Students listen again and match the suggestions with the responses. You may need to stop the CD occasionally to allow students to record their answers.

> **Answers**
> 1 d   2 f   3 e   4 a   5 c   6 b

Feedback focus

Point out that in response b, *Let's …* is another way of making a suggestion.

4 Ask the students to study the responses and say which are used to accept and which to reject suggestions.

> **Answers**
> b, c, e, and f accept; a and d reject.

Pronunciation

Make sure the students say the responses with the appropriate intonation. In particular, the ones which reject suggestions need to be said tactfully. Use the recording of the conversation as a model if they are having problems.

Unit 8 Orders

45

5 Students make and respond to suggestions in pairs.

Watch out! Students will need to change *we* to *you* in some of the suggestions. (NB *Shall you ...?* is not possible.) Point out that *What / How about ...* is followed by a verb in the *-ing* form. Students may want to say **I suggest you to ...* on the pattern of *I advise you to ...* Point out that *suggest* is followed by subject + verb (as in *I suggest we use* from the conversation) or a verb in the *-ing* form (e.g. *I suggest sending an email ...*).

Possible answers
2 **A** Let's send an email to all our customers.
    B Fine. And then we could send a flyer the next week.
3 **A** Why don't you ask for a pay rise?
    B I don't think that will work. We only get pay rises once a year.
4 **A** I suggest we look for a new supplier on the Internet.
    B OK. Can you do that?
5 **A** You look tired. Maybe you should leave early tonight.
    B I'm not sure about that. I've got lots of work to finish.
6 **A** How about having a weekly meeting to talk about our problems?
    B Yes, I think we should do that. Let's meet on a Friday afternoon.

Extra activity

Students write down a problem (real or fictional) they have. The students mingle and must ask up to six other students for suggestions for their problem. They write down the advice they receive. In open class, the students describe their problem, and say which advice they liked or didn't like.

» If students need more practice, go to **Practice file 8** on page 116 of the **Student's Book**.

6 Give students plenty of time to think up ideas before they start speaking (for example, for homework). This will make the discussion more animated and produce more practice of the target language. Students discuss their ideas for the canteen in pairs or small groups. Encourage maximum use of the language from **3**. Ask the students to read through the *Key expressions*. At the end, students present their ideas to the class.

Alternative

Write the expressions from **3** on pieces of card. Include two examples of each expression. Make one set of cards for each group. The cards are spread on the table in front of the students, who can take a card when they have used that expression. The student with the most cards at the end is the winner. Another variation is to have one student as an invigilator who ticks off the expressions as they are used.

One-to-one

The student and you discuss the situation together. Make sure the student has the chance to both make and respond to suggestions.

ⓘ Refer students to the **Interactive Workbook Email** and **Phrasebank** sections for further study and to the **Exercises and Tests** for revision.

Case study

Background

This *Case study* presents a situation where a company is reinventing itself in response to the challenge of a new technology (in this case, the Internet) changing the way customers want to do business. For certain kinds of goods (in this case, electrical / computer goods), customers seem more inclined to buy online, and high street stores such as Dixons need to adapt to this new environment. However, if an online retailer is to prosper, its delivery systems need to be excellent, and so the choice of a delivery company is crucial. In this *Case study*, the students are required to use different criteria to assess delivery companies, and decide which one to use.

The *Task* is in three parts: listening to an expert to find out which characteristics are important when choosing a delivery company; a reading activity to assess the advantages and disadvantages of a company; and finally a meeting to pool information about three different companies and decide which to use.

Discussion

As a lead-in, review the text about Amazon and UPS at the start of the unit, including the characteristics of UPS that have made it so useful to Amazon's operation. Then ask students to read about Dixons and answer the questions, which can be discussed in open class, or in small groups.

> **Answers**
> 1 Because of the crisis in the retail industry
> 2 Suggested: quick response times, reliable service (especially sending the right goods in the correct condition), politeness to customers, good response to complaints, competitive prices
> 3 Suggested: reliability and speed of delivery, ability to track orders, different delivery options, low prices

Watch out! You may wish to pre-teach the following.
leading = main, most important
retailer = company which sells to the public

Task

1 42▷ This listening follows on closely from question 3 in *Discussion*. Students listen to the expert and number the characteristics in the order they hear them.

> **Answers**
> 1 price
> 2 speed of delivery
> 3 tracking system
> 4 delivery options
> 5 first time delivery rate

Extension

Ask students to write down what, according to the expert, is the key to choosing a delivery company. (Answer: finding a balance between price and reliability.) This will be useful for the discussions which follow.

2 Divide the class into three groups, and call the groups A, B, and C. If you have extra students 'left over', they should join an existing group. If you are teaching one-to-two, make yourself the C. Each group reads their respective file. They discuss the advantages and disadvantages of 'their' company: explain that for some of the items (e.g. price) the students will not know if this is a plus or a minus point until they have discussed the other files.

One-to-one

The student should read all three Files, and you and he / she discuss the three companies together.

3 Make new groups of three with an A, B, and C from each of the old groups. You could ask students to make separate presentations on the advantages and disadvantages of their company, but it may be more realistic to ask students to go through each item in the File and compare the three companies. At the end, in order to practise the language of suggestions, ask the students (still in their groups) to discuss and decide what they are going to do.

Extra activity

For students who need to practise presentation skills, you could ask them to prepare a formal presentation to make to the group (including visuals) about which company they have chosen, and why.

》 Unit 8 **Progress test** and **Speaking test**, pages 102–103.

Unit 8 | Orders

47

9 | Selling

Unit content

By the end of this unit, students will be able to
- talk about sales and advertising
- talk about advertising laws using modal verbs
- interrupt or avoid interruption
- control the discussion in meetings.

Context

The quality of a product or service is often virtually irrelevant if the company hasn't thought about how to sell it. This means thinking about advertising and marketing, product placement, offers and discounts, targeting the right market segment, and many more factors. Enormous sums of money are spent on researching which products or services to sell in which market, the best way to sell it, and advertising campaigns, not all of which are guaranteed success. Sometimes, products seem to benefit from *lack* of advertising, succeeding by word-of-mouth and personal recommendation. In fact, it seems that the canniest campaigns are the ones which make the consumer feel there has been no campaign. All companies wish to increase their sales, so all business people are involved, directly or indirectly, in selling.

This involvement will often mean that employees are required to take part in meetings. This can be a particularly difficult situation for the non-native speaker, so having the tools to control a meeting or be able to interject successfully is vital to non-native speakers of English.

This unit presents the language of sales and advertising, and gives students ample chance to discuss the issues surrounding it. It also presents useful language for participating in meetings and controlling discussions. The unit ends with a *Case study* where the students discuss how to promote a new product.

Starting point

You could start by showing various advertisements on video or in magazines. Ask what they are for, and whether the students think they work. Then students discuss the questions in small groups.

Working with words

Extra activity

Ask students to close their books. Then read out the following numbers and dates and ask students to write them down.
  1995   €2 billion   5%   30-40%   2006
Students then open their books and scan the text to find out what each number refers to.

1 Students read the text and answer the questions. They can discuss their answers with a partner.

> **Answers**
> 1 True 2 False 3 False 4 True 5 True

2 Students make useful phrases. Then they check with the article.

> **Answers**
> 1 h (a and g are also possible) 2 d 3 b 4 f 5 g 6 c 7 e 8 a

3 Students look back at **2** and work out the meanings of the verbs.

> **Answers**
> a 3b
> b 2d
> c 7e
> d 1h, 5g, 8a
> e 4f

4 Students look back at **2** and work out the meanings of the words and phrases.

> **Answers**
> 1 an advertising campaign 3 a discount
> 2 range   4 market share

5 Students complete the questions with verbs from **2**.

> **Answers**
> 1 enter   4 expanded
> 2 boost   5 launch
> 3 attract
> 1 In 1995
> 2 It put live fish in its supermarkets.
> 3 By putting frozen fish in supermarkets away from the sea.
> 4 It has introduced loyalty cards and provided credit.
> 5 An advertising campaign for online shopping.

Tip Refer students to the *Tip* about *ad, advert, advertisement,* and *advertising*.

Watch out! Note the word stress.
ad*ver*tisement (British English) advert*is*ement (US English)
*ad*vert *ad*vertising

6 To prepare students for the activity, ask students to list all the different kinds of advertising they see (e.g. junk mail, billboards). You may need to provide vocabulary. They then study the photos and match them to three of the phrases in the box. Check the students understand the meaning of all six items.

Answers
1 Outdoor advertising 2 Direct mailing 3 Word-of-mouth

7 Students discuss the questions in pairs and then in open class.

Possible answers
Because it is seen as more credible by customers, it costs the company very little and doesn't depend on activity by the company to keep it going.
It is not true if a company artificially tries to start a word-of-mouth campaign, and gets found out. If you get bad word-of-mouth, it spreads more quickly than good.

» If students need more practice, go to **Practice file 9** on page 118 of the **Student's Book.**

8 Students work in pairs and small groups to discuss the questions. Encourage use of the language studied so far in this unit.

Feedback focus
You may need to feed in extra ways of advertising not mentioned so far in this unit, e.g. product placement in films, getting a 'buzz' going on sites like YouTube.

Pre-work learners
Instead of question 2, ask your students to do some research outside the classroom: students choose a new product area, and find out the different ways this product is advertised in the real world. They bring their findings back to class and exchange with other students.

ⓘ Refer students to the **Interactive Workbook Glossary** for further study.

Language at work

1 Ask the students what they know about São Paulo. Students discuss the headline and photo, then read the text and answer the questions.

Answers
1 There is no billboard advertising.
2 Students' own answers

2 Students put the verbs in bold in the table.

Answers for 2 and 3
It's necessary	need to / have to
It's not necessary	don't have to / don't need to
It's possible / permitted	can / are allowed to
It's not possible / permitted	can't / aren't allowed to

Pronunciation
Make sure students pronounce (1) the weak form in *to* /tə/ (2) *have to* correctly /hæf tuː/.

3 Students add the two new forms to the table.

Answers
See above

4 43▷ Students listen to the four speakers and match them to the statements. They could write down key words they heard, and compare their answers with their partner.

Watch out! As this activity practises listening for gist, do not pre-teach vocabulary.

Answers
a 3 b 4 c 1 d 2

5 43▷ Students complete the sentences and then listen to check.

Answers
1 have to   6 are allowed to, can't
2 don't need to   7 don't have to
3 need to   8 can
4 have to   9 don't have to
5 aren't allowed to

Watch out! Students may ask you about *must* and *mustn't*. *Must* is another way of expressing obligation (usually coming from the speaker rather than from a law or a regulation) and is similar to *have to*. *Mustn't* (pronounced /mʌsˈnt/) expresses a prohibition, and is similar to *aren't allowed to*.

6 Give students time to study the notices. You could ask them where they might see them. Students work in pairs and interpret the notices using the verbs in **2**.

Unit 9 | Selling

49

> **Suggested answers**
> 2 You have to pay by card. / You can only pay by card. / You aren't allowed to pay by cash.
> 3 You need / have to reply before 31st October to benefit … / If you reply before … you can benefit …
> 4 You can't / are not allowed to change or cancel this ticket.
> 5 You can / are allowed to pay by credit card. / You don't have / need to pay by cash.
> 6 You can't / aren't allowed to advertise here.

» If students need more practice, go to **Practice file 9** on page 119 of the **Student's Book**.

7 Ask students to read the instructions carefully, and check understanding of the vocabulary. They should spend a few minutes thinking which question form is most appropriate for each item. Point out the formation of the questions (students may want to say *Have you to …?*): drill a couple of examples if necessary. Students work in pairs and small groups to answer the questions. Encourage use of the modal verbs from **2**.

Feedback focus
Monitor for correct use of the modal verbs; also the use of the verb *be* with *allowed to* and the pronunciation of *have to*.

Extra activity
If you think students need more practice in this area, ask them to discuss rules and regulations in their countries. Topics could include: laws for under-18s, voting and elections, driving (both cars and motorcycles), drinking alcohol, travelling to other countries / visas. NB make sure you choose topics which are acceptable in your local teaching context.

Practically speaking

1 44▷ Teach *relocation*. Ask students why companies relocate, and if they have personal experience of it. They listen and answer the questions.

> **Answers**
> 1 Relocating to low-cost countries such as China
> 2 No

2 44▷ The students listen again, and record the order in which the phrases are said.

> **Answers**
> The correct order is 5 – 4 – 3 – 1 – 2.

3 Students read the phrases and decide their function.

> **Answers**
> 1 Can I just say something here? / Sorry, but …
> 2 Please let me finish. / Can I just finish?
> 3 Sorry, go ahead.

4 Give students plenty of time to think of ideas for this discussion, so that the discussion goes on long enough for them to use the phrases from **3**. They should write down three or four ideas for each topic. In pairs, they talk about each topic and practise interrupting each other.

Watch out! Interrupting is considered rude in many countries and in any case, some students are too shy or polite to do it! It can sometimes help if the students 'take on' a new identity for such discussions: if they pretend to be (say) American, they may find it easier.

Alternative
To make sure the discussion does not stop too soon, say that the winner is the person talking after five minutes.

Alternative
Students who are interrupted toss a coin: if it's heads, they use an expression to ask to finish, and continue to speak. If tails, they let the other person speak.

Business communication

Extra activity
Ask students if they have many meetings in their companies, and what they like / dislike about them. Elicit problems that business people often quote about meetings (too long, not focused enough, some participants talk too much) and explain that controlling the discussion (the focus of this section) is an important skill, as it can reduce these problems.

Pre-work learners
Ask the students what they think the problems might be with meetings in companies.

1 45▷ As this listening is quite long, you may wish to break it into three sections and ask students to compare answers after each section. Students listen to the meeting and complete the notes.

Answers
Advertising:
- Money spent last year: €28.6 million
- Budget this year: €37.5 million
- Extra money to be used for: **a big outdoor advertising campaign**

Sales:
- This year + **7–10** %
- Next two years: + **7–10** %
- Key markets: the Czech Republic, **Poland, Hungary**

2 45▷ Teach *follow-up*. You may need to explain or elicit the meanings of sentences 1–6 before students can match up with a–f.

Answers
1 f   2 c   3 e   4 d   5 b   6 a

Watch out! The sentences contain a number of phrasal and / or idiomatic verbs which students may not know.
catch = understand, hear
get off (the subject) = leave a subject (to talk about something else)
cover = deal with
I'm not with you = I don't follow what you're saying.
sum up = describe the important facts about something
move on (to) = start a new topic
come back to = return to a topic
You could ask students to look these up in a dictionary, or guess their meaning from the audio script on page 154 of the Student's Book. NB the meanings are also addressed in **3**.

3 The students write the phrases from **2** next to the functions.

Answers
1 1f   4 3e
2 2c   5 4d
3 5b   6 6a

Pronunciation
Make sure students say the phrases with the correct stress and intonation (particularly important with these functional phrases):
We're <u>here</u> to<u>day</u> to talk about … We need to dis<u>cuss</u> …
<u>Sorry</u>, I didn't <u>catch</u> that … <u>what</u> was that you <u>said</u>?
<u>Sorry</u> I'm not <u>with</u> you … could you be more spe<u>cific</u>?
We're getting <u>off</u> the <u>subject</u> … can we come <u>back</u> to that <u>later</u>?
OK, I <u>think</u> we've covered <u>everything</u> … can we move <u>on</u> to the <u>next</u> point?
I <u>think</u> that's <u>everything</u> … can we sum <u>up</u> what we've a<u>greed</u>?

4 Students work in pairs: Student A says the sentences and Student B gives responses from **2**.

Alternative
Students work in groups of three. Student A says a sentence, Student B responds with one of the phrases from **2**, and Student C with another.

» If students need more practice, go to **Practice file 9** on page 118 of the **Student's Book**.

5 Ask students to study the *Key expressions*. Check meaning and pronunciation. Explain that the objective of this role-play is to use the new language as much as possible rather than 'win' the meeting. If numbers dictate, ask students to take more than one role. As with previous role-plays, you could have the sentences on cards on the table, which students pick up as they say them – this makes it more fun, and encourages use of the language. In order to get good output of the new language, make sure the meetings go on for a reasonable length of time. Stronger groups should be encouraged to include interrupting language from *Practically speaking*.

Feedback focus
Monitor for correct use of the sentences from this section, including natural stress, rhythm, and intonation. Bring common mistakes to the students' attention at the end of the meeting.

ⓘ Refer students to the **Interactive Workbook Email** and **Phrasebank** sections for further study and to the **Exercises and Tests** for revision.

Unit 9 | Selling

Case study

Background

Businesses are always looking at ways to exploit the increased spending power of young people. Since they are also the greatest users of the Internet, this is the obvious medium for advertising directed at the young, which is the focus of the *Case study*.

In addition, young people watch, play, and communicate over a range of media – they watch TV but also clips of programmes on video sites; they talk to their friends through chatsites, emails, text messages, and mobiles; they play games on PlayStations, on PCs, and online. This means that companies have to be flexible in choosing media on which to promote their products.

Finally, young people are very savvy about manipulation by other people. Companies must present their promotions in a way that does not 'turn off' young people.

In the *Task*, students are required to devise a promotional campaign for a credit card for young people. In the first part, they read various ideas for the campaign, then pool the ideas and decide on a strategy.

As a lead-in, especially if your students are young, conduct a quick questionnaire about their online habits:

How many hours do you spend online per week?

How often do you communicate with friends online?

About how many contacts do you have in your online community?

What do you usually talk about when you are communicating online?

What is the most popular pastime for young people?

Elicit why the youth market is so important and whether any of the students work for companies that sell in that market. If so, how do they promote their products?

Students read the *Background* text and answer the questions.

Discussion

The questions can be discussed in open class, or in small groups.

Answers
1 To reach the youth market
2 and 3 Students' own answers

Task

1 Students read the instructions carefully. Check they understand the situation. Put them into groups of three, with each student reading a different File.

2 Students meet and discuss the twelve options in the Files. Encourage students to use the language of interrupting and controlling the discussion. Students decide which of the ideas to adopt (within the budget) and when to start each one.

One-to-one

Your student should read Files 18 and 43, while you read File 55. As with the previous meeting role-play, you may need to speak deliberately quickly, or try to change the subject, etc. in order to elicit the meetings language from the student.

» Unit 9 **Progress test** and **Speaking test**, pages 104–105.

10 | New ideas

Unit content

By the end of this unit, students will be able to
- talk about new green initiatives
- talk about innovative practices using the passive
- ask for clarification
- give a formal presentation.

Context

Until relatively recently, mainstream business has tended to avoid the issue of the environment, or even been hostile to the idea that companies should 'go green'. This is changing rapidly, as managers have realized the financial and public relations benefits of a greener approach to business, so much so that most companies, large and small, pay at least lip service to their environmental credentials. Partly this is because consumers are less and less inclined to use a company which has a reputation for being anti-green: so a company will lose business unless it can show how green it is. If you type 'making business green' into an Internet search engine, you will get more than eight million hits.

To some extent, one's attitude to green issues is cultural. For example, northern European countries such as Germany or Denmark have traditionally been at the forefront of making business green; developing countries have taken the understandable viewpoint that restrictions on output or distribution are going to hit them hard just as they are gaining market share. So your students are likely to express differing viewpoints, depending on where they come from, and what business they are in.

A final point is that many businesses have sprung up around the green issue: some of them feature in this unit. The two fields are inextricably entwined.

This unit provides the opportunity to discuss environmental issues within the business world and to learn useful vocabulary in that field. It also gives a basic introduction to the language of presentations and gives students ample chance to practise. They will also practise asking for clarification. The unit ends with a *Case study* where students discuss improving the green image of a company and make a presentation.

Starting point

Allow the students time to consider their responses to the questions. Students discuss them in small groups, and then feed back to class. Be prepared for a wide range of opinions.

Pre-work learners

In question 1, change *company* to *school / college*.

Working with words

1 Students study the photo and discuss briefly what GreenCitizen might provide. Then they read the text quickly and check.

> **Answer**
> It disposes of old computers for companies.

2 Students read the text again more carefully, and discuss the questions with their partner. Don't do too much work on the vocabulary of the text at this point, as this is the focus of **3**.

> **Answers**
> 1 Because they could pay a fine if they do not respect the environment.
> 2 It uses only registered recycling companies.
> 3 They can maintain an environmentally-friendly image when they update their systems. It is convenient and good value for money.

3 Students find words in the text that correspond to the quotes. You may need to add further explanations and examples, as the quotes are not exact definitions.

> **Answers**
> 1 affordable
> 2 convenient
> 3 new initiative
> 4 good value for money
> 5 recycling
> 6 environmentally friendly
> 7 disposal
> 8 original

4 In pairs: Student A reads out a phrase in bold from the text, and Student B defines it.

Tip Refer students to the *Tip* about *green*.

5 46▷ Use the photos to pre-teach vocabulary (see below). Students describe the photos briefly, then listen to do the matching.

Watch out! You might need to pre-teach the following.
reverse vending machine = a machine where you can also put the can back into the machine when you have finished your drink
waste / rubbish = things you throw away
canteen = company restaurant / cafeteria
biodegradable = able to disappear into nature naturally
harmful = causing damage
carpooling = sharing a car to get to work

Unit 10 | New ideas

53

take part = do an activity with other people, participate
carbon emissions = the sending out of carbon (especially carbon dioxide) into the atmosphere

> **Answers**
> a 3   b 2   c 4   d 1

6 46▷ Students listen again and complete the table.

> **Answers**
>
> | Speaker | Green initiative | Advantages |
> |---|---|---|
> | 1 | reverse vending machine | 1 you feel like you're helping the environment |
> | | | 2 the office produces less waste |
> | 2 | turning lights off | 1 saves energy |
> | | | 2 cuts costs |
> | 3 | biodegradable cups, etc. | 1 teaches people about green issues |
> | | | 2 makes rubbish less harmful to the environment |
> | 4 | carpooling | 1 cuts emissions by more than half |
> | | | 2 people don't arrive so late |

7 Students match the adjectives to the meanings, and say which initiative they refer to.

> **Answers**
> 1 c – reverse vending machine
> 2 d – biodegradable cups, etc.
> 3 b – carpooling
> 4 a – turning lights off

» If students need more practice, go to **Practice file 10** on page 120 of the **Student's Book**.

8 Students discuss the four initiatives. Ask if any of them are in place in their own places of work or study, and / or whether they would be feasible. What might the disadvantages be of each?

9 Students should form pairs from different companies if possible, and find out what their partner's company does.

Pre-work learners

For questions 1 and 2, students should discuss their place of study. They could write a letter to their principal, suggesting new green initiatives the school could take.

ⓘ Refer students to the **Interactive Workbook Glossary** for further study.

Language at work

1 Ask students to describe the photo. Explain the acronyms *G1G1* (= Give one get one), *OLPC* (= one laptop per child), and *XO* (= the brand name of the laptop). Ask the students if they have heard of or used this laptop. Students read the text and answer the questions.

> **Answers**
> 1 The laptop cost more to produce than the selling price.
> 2 It uses little power, it can be charged by solar panels, the screen can be used in the sun, there are no moveable parts.
> 3 For each laptop sold in the USA, one was given to a child in an underdeveloped country.

Extra activity

To improve the students' ability to read texts without using a dictionary, ask them to find words in the text which mean the following (answers given in brackets).
 a went up (*rose*)
 b supply, sending out (*distribution*)
 c had an idea (*came up with*)
 d now (*currently*)
 e evaluate (*judge*)

2 Students complete the sentences.

> **Answers**
> 1 is aimed   3 were sold
> 2 are produced   4 was given

3 Students complete the rules using the sentences in **2** to help.

> **Answers**
> 2 be   3 is   4 were

Tip Refer students to the *Tip* about *by*. You could point out that we use *in* to say where something is made / produced: *The computers are made in Taiwan.*

» If students need more practice, go to **Practice file 10** on page 121 of the **Student's Book**.

4 47▷ Elicit / teach *outsourcing* (= paying another company to do some of your company's work). Ask students to give examples, and if they have experience of it. Go through the instructions and the table carefully with the students. Tell them they do not need to worry about the verbs in brackets for now. Students listen to the recording and tick the services which are outsourced.

Watch out! You might need to pre-teach the following.
contract (vb) = make an agreement / contract to do something

54

Answers (for 4 and 5)

	Advertising agency		Pharmaceutical company	
	Outsourced?	Reason	Outsourced?	Reason
Cleaning	✓	Building is so big	✗	Machines need to be cleaned by professionals
Maintenance	✓	Costs less	✗	Need experts to look after the machines
IT	✗	Programs are so specialized	✓	Don't have many computers
Human Resources	✗	HR department is quite big	✓	Only 50 employees
Training	✓	So much training it has to be outsourced	✓	Don't need it very often
Food + catering	✓	To get a better service	✓	Only a few employees use the service

5 47▷ Students listen again and complete the reasons columns.

> **Answers**
> See above

6 Students use the information in the table to make sentences in the passive. Monitor carefully for the correct formation of the passive.

7 Students work in pairs to discuss the questions. Encourage use of the passive, using the examples in **6**.

Pre-work learners

Students could talk about the services in their school or college (cleaning, catering, IT). Or they could imagine they are working for a company and invent the details.

Extension

Ask students to compare outsourcing across the class: for example, is it more common in some countries than others? If your students work in the public sector (e.g. hospitals), ask if services such as cleaning are outsourced to private companies, and how this is seen by employees or customers.

Practically speaking

1 48▷ Teach *clarification*. Students listen to the conversation and underline the correct answers.

> **Answers**
> 1 the whole company   3 can't
> 2 next year   4 agrees

2 48▷ Students listen again and complete the sentences.

> **Answers**
> 1 Do you mean   3 Are you saying
> 2 Sorry, did you say   4 What do you mean by

3 Students work in pairs and use the prompts to practise the phrases. The other student should give an appropriate answer.

> **Possible answers**
> 1 Do you mean the 21st or the 31st of October?
> 2 Sorry, did you say all our customers or just our VIP customers?
> 3 Are you saying we should cancel all our orders with that supplier?
> 4 Do you mean 15 or 50?
> 5 Sorry, did you say the staff on the first floor or all the staff?

Pronunciation

In the questions with two alternatives, make sure students use contrastive stress correctly.
1 *Do you mean the twenty-first or the thirty-first of October?*
2 *Did you say all our customers or just our VIP customers?*
4 *Do you mean fifteen or fifty?*
5 *Did you say the staff on the first floor or all the staff?*

Business communication

1 This activity revises vocabulary from earlier in the unit. You could write some of the words and phrases on the board. Students should make a list of advantages for use in **2**.

> **Possible answers**
> Green policies can save money (by recycling goods or cutting bills) and increase profits / raise awareness of green issues among staff / make the company environmentally friendly to the public / more attractive to job applicants / create a feelgood factor amongst the staff / help to save the world.

Unit 10 | New ideas

55

2 49▷ Students listen to the presentation and complete the notes. They also compare the notes with the advantages they wrote down in **1**.

Answers
1 profits
2 customers
3 employer
4 regulations

3 49▷ Students match the beginnings and ends of the sentences from the presentation, then listen again to check their answers (or read the audio script on pages 154–155).

Answers
1 f   2 e   3 h   4 g   5 a   6 c   7 d   8 b

4 Explain that the phrases in **3** are all useful for structuring a presentation. Elicit why this might be important. (Answer: because it helps the listeners to understand the content, especially if they are non-native speakers). Students match the phrases to the categories.

Answers
1   1, 3
2   4, 5
3   2, 6
4   7, 8

5 Ask students what *ebilling* is and whether they pay any bills in this way. Elicit advantages and disadvantages for both company and customer. Put students into pairs and ask them to read through the instructions and notes. Check vocabulary. Students take turns to give a rough presentation using the notes and the phrases from **4**. Monitor but do not interrupt.

Alternative

Student A in each pair says the first word or two of each phrase, and Student B must complete it. If they are still struggling, write slashed sentences on the board:
I / here / today / tell / benefits / green.

Feedback focus

Focus on the structure and organization of the presentations, and the use of the target language, rather than grammatical or pronunciation mistakes.

» If students need more practice, go to **Practice file 10** on page 120 of the **Student's Book**.

6 Students conclude the section by making a formal presentation. Put the students in pairs, with Student A reading File 19, and Student B reading File 44. They should also study the *Key expressions*. Students use the information in the Files to make a presentation to each other. The listener should take notes.

Pronunciation

When students are nervous, their delivery can become monotonous and 'machine-gun-like'. To avoid this, encourage them to divide their sentences into chunks of meaning (usually no more than seven words), with each chunk having one main stress on the most important word, and a very slight pause between the chunks. Here is an example from **6**:
This is not a problem // for our corporate customers // but for private users // especially older people // it could be an issue.
(// = a pause)

Feedback focus

Ask the Student As to work in pairs and small groups and compare (a) the notes they took (b) the organization and delivery of the presentations they listened to. Student Bs do the same.

Extra activity

Confident students could give their presentations to the whole class. They could be videoed and analysed later by the class.

One-to-one

The student makes one or both of the presentations. You take notes and the student compares your notes with the original File.

ⓘ Refer students to the **Interactive Workbook Email** and **Phrasebank** sections for further study and to the **Exercises and Tests** for revision.

Case study

Background

This *Case study* focuses on how companies can reduce their carbon footprint and improve their green image. As shown already in this unit, companies are increasingly aware and active in this area, for reasons of both public relations and concrete financial benefits. In the *Task*, the students are required to discuss different ideas for making their company greener, and decide which ones are best. An in-work class can be encouraged to compare the ideas presented here with what happens in their real-life companies.

As a lead-in, ask the students if they know of any green initiatives by companies (perhaps in their own country). Are they being followed for reasons of PR, financial benefit, or genuine concern for the environment?

Students then read the text about the three companies.

Discussion

The questions can be discussed in open class, or in small groups. You will probably find considerable disagreement (even scientists disagree) and the answers to questions 1 and 2, in particular, change as more research is done. For question 3, you might like to guide their discussion into the three areas in the Files: transport, resources, and energy.

> **Possible answers**
> 1 Students' own answers.
> 2 The burning of fossil fuels (including industry and transport) and deforestation / Use of CFCs in refrigeration systems / Use of fertilizers in agriculture
> 3 **Transport:** use public transport rather than cars and planes; carpooling; drive at an efficient speed; combine trips when flying
> **Resources:** reuse and recycle; do more things online to save paper; take showers rather than baths; plant trees
> **Energy:** switch off lights and computer monitors; insulate your house; dry your clothes outside in the wind and not in a machine; carbon offsetting

Task

1 Put the students into three groups. Explain that all the students work for the same company. You may want to specify some information about the company (how big it is, what it produces, what kind of buildings it has, etc.) in order to make the students' discussion more focused. Explain that each group will be dealing with a particular aspect of the green issue. Each group reads their respective File.

Students then discuss and make notes on what the company can do in their area. They may need some time to think up ideas. Do not hurry them at this stage, as the ideas will be essential for the discussion in **2**.

2 Students prepare a presentation about what they have decided. Make sure all students take notes. Now make new groups of three with one student from each area. Each student gives their presentation to the new group.

Alternative

Instead of groups of three, make groups of six, with two students from each area, who make a joint presentation. This will increase collaboration and reduce stress. Make sure students decide before the presentation who is going to do which bit.

3 Students discuss all the ideas, either in their new groups of three (or six) or in open class. They decide which initiatives the company is going to adopt.

One-to-one

The student could use their own company as the model, if feasible. He or she reads one of the Files and makes the presentation. He or she then reads the other Files (or listens to a presentation by you about them). You and he or she then discuss the ideas and decide together.

» Unit 10 **Progress test** and **Speaking test**, pages 106–107.

11 Entertaining

Unit content

By the end of this unit, students will be able to
- talk about corporate entertainment
- talk about future possibilities using the first conditional
- talk about food and drink
- make and respond to invitations and offers.

Context

Corporate entertainment has expanded considerably in recent years. Although the idea of companies 'wining and dining' their clients is well-established, this area of business life has now spawned its own companies who exist simply to provide entertainment and hospitality services for business people. The events fall into two categories: ones which are used to build and reinforce relationships with people outside the company – usually clients, but also service providers, agents, writers, and so on. These tend to be social and sporting events (often involving a lot of eating and drinking): the new Wembley Stadium in London has 18,000 corporate seats. The second type of event is provided for the company's own staff, usually to increase team-building or motivation. These often involve games like paintballing or problem-solving activities like murder mystery weekends.

Corporate hospitality is now a massive industry in itself – currently about £1 billion a year in the UK and set to rise dramatically for the 2012 Olympics. There is no doubt that the recipients of hospitality enjoy and appreciate it, though whether it makes much difference to clients' decision-making is another matter. In any case, food and drink is an important part of the business person's life.

In this unit, students will start by talking about corporate entertainment. Most contact between business people from different companies will involve food and drink, and the language to discuss it will be immediately useful. Within this context the language of inviting and accepting or declining an invitation is key, and students are given a number of take-away expressions to help them with it. The *Case study* at the end of the unit involves organizing a successful corporate event.

Starting point

Explain / elicit briefly *corporate entertainment*. Allow the students time to consider their responses to the questions. Then discuss the questions in open class, or small groups.

Pronunciation

Make sure students pronounce the section title correctly.
corporate /ˈkɔːrpərət/ *entertainment*

Working with words

1 Students describe the photos, and explain the link to corporate entertainment. Ask if any of the students have organized or attended such events for their work. They read the text and find seven examples of corporate entertainment.

> **Answers**
> concerts / golf / wine-tasting cruises / watching sumo wrestling / parachute jumping / paintballing / a night at the opera

2 Students work in pairs to answer the questions.

> **Answers**
> 1 major sports and cultural events / because many tickets are bought for corporate enetertainment
> 2 to improve relationships with customers, suppliers, or staff
> 3 possible answers: budget, location, choosing an event which suits the customer

Watch out! You might wish to pre-teach the following.
VIPs = very important people
tool = something that helps you do something
cruise = pleasure trip on a boat
paintballing = action combat game where you try to shoot other players with paint

3 Students complete the table with vocabulary in bold from the text.

> **Answers**
> (In order) host company – guests – purpose – venue – event – budget

4 50▷ Students listen and complete the table.

Watch out! You might need to pre-teach the following.
dealer = someone who sells goods for a company
convention = large meeting
quad bikes = four-wheel motorbikes with large tyres
fortune = large amount of money

Answers

	1	2
Host company	Spanish electronics company	German bank
Guests	dealers in Spain	VIP clients
Purpose	reinforce relationship between company and clients	entertain its clients
Venue	5-star hotel in Brazil	La Scala opera house
Events	tourist visits, riding quad bikes	Opera (Tristan and Isolde)

5 50▷ Students make the phrases, then listen to check.

Answers
1 f 2 d 3 e 4 a 5 c 6 b

6 Students match the phrases in **5** to the meanings.

Answers
a reinforce a relationship   d arrange a trip
b accept an invitation   e book a venue
c entertain clients   f hold an event

Extra activity
Ask students to list other collocations with these verbs.
Possible answers
  book + tickets, flights, a restaurant, a hotel, a court (for tennis)
  reinforce + a reputation, a stereotype, a building
  arrange + a meeting, a party, a conference, a loan, an appointment
  entertain + friends, guests, the audience, the crowd
  hold + a party, a meeting, a reservation, office, an opinion, a conversation
  accept + a proposal, an offer, a bribe, the job, money, advice

7 Students test each other in pairs.

» If students need more practice, go to **Practice file 11** on page 122 of the **Student's Book**.

  Tip Refer students to the *Tip* about *customer* and *client*.

8 Students work in small groups to plan a corporate event for one of the companies. Point out that the type of company and the nature of the guests will impact on the size and type of event: motivational events tend to have more games and fewer cultural activities, while events for VIPs will be high-status (and budget). Groups should report back on their discussions briefly.

9 Students discuss the questions in pairs. Feed back briefly to class.

Pre-work learners
Students should discuss the second question only.

ⓘ Refer students to the **Interactive Workbook Glossary** for further study.

Language at work

1 Ask students if they ever have to take clients out for a meal (or are taken out). What makes you choose a particular restaurant? (Often the level of the restaurant depends on the usefulness of the client to the company.)

2 51▷ Give the students a few minutes to study the table. They listen and complete the table.

Answers
1 seafood   3 live jazz on Thursday
2 €60 a head   4 7.00

3 51▷ Students underline the correct form, then listen and check.

Answers
1 's, 'll be able   3 go, 'll be
2 choose, 'll cost   4 won't be, get

Pronunciation
Make sure students pronounce the negative *won't* correctly /wəʊnt/, and they can discriminate *won't* and *want* /wɒnt/.

4 Students study the sentences in **2**, then complete the rules.

Answers
1 future   3 comma
2 present, verb without 'to'

5 Students work in pairs, and ask and answer questions using the situations.

Answers
2 A How will you get there if your flight is cancelled?
  B We'll rent a car.
3 A How will the staff react if your company closes a department?
  B I think they'll be very worried.
4 A What will the benefits be if your company changes location?
  B It'll be easier to park.
5 A What will happen if you change your job?
  B I'll earn more money.

Unit 11 | Entertaining

Pronunciation

For students who need a high level of pronunciation, encourage them to contract *What will* to *What'll* (rhyming with *bottle*).

» If students need more practice, go to **Practice file 11** on page 123 of the **Student's Book**.

Feedback focus

Focus on correct use of the first conditional and pronunciation of *won't*.

6 Students ask and answer using the prompts.

> **Suggested answers**
> 2 A What will you do if you don't get a pay rise soon?
>   B I'll probably find another job.
> 3 A What will your company do if it makes a large profit next year?
>   B I don't know, but we'll probably get a bonus.
> 4 A What will you do at the weekend if it's sunny?
>   B I'll probably go to the beach.

Extension

Stronger students could use *could / might* in place of *will*: *We might get a bonus*.

Pre-work learners

Change questions 1 and 3 to:
1 headteacher – fail your exams
3 school – everybody passes their exams.

Practically speaking

1 52▷ Students study the waiter's notebook. Elicit / explain the dishes. Point out to any shocked Italian students that pasta is often a main course in the UK. Students listen and tick the choices for each section.

> **Answers**
> The following should be ticked:
> Parma ham and salad, spaghetti and lasagne, white wine

2 52▷ Students listen again and match the questions to the responses.

> **Answers**
> 1 b   2 c   3 a

Tip Refer students to the *Tip* about *the*.

3 52▷ Students practise saying the phrases in **2**, and underline the stressed words.

> **Answers**
> 1 What do you recommend? You must try the Parma ham.
> 2 What are the pizzas like? They're not bad, but I recommend the pasta.
> 3 What are you having? I think I'll have the lasagne.

Pronunciation

Students may wish to know some basic rules for sentence stress:
  a we usually stress the key information words – these will often be verbs, nouns, or adjectives: *He works for Ford*.
  b we can stress other words if there is a special meaning to get across:
    These radios are made near Tokyo. (i.e. not in Tokyo)
    These radios are made near Tokyo. (but other ones are made in Taiwan)
  c we stress new information, and never old information:
    I bought a car. A green car.

4 Make sure one student is the 'expert' who has been to the restaurant before.

Feedback focus

Focus on the use of the phrases from **2**, and the use of *the*.

Extension

Make the activity into a role-play. Arrange the tables to make a 'restaurant' and appoint a student to be the waiter. Ask the waiter to be quite slow, to give the 'diners' a chance to discuss the menu, and also make small talk while they are waiting. Use the role-play to recycle functional language from this book: making polite requests (Unit 1), showing interest (Unit 4), making small talk and developing a conversation (Unit 7).

Business communication

1 53▷ Students listen and match the conversations to the places.

Answers
a 1   b 3   c 2   d 4

2 53▷ Depending on how good their memory is, students may need to listen to the conversations again before doing the exercise. Students complete all eight sentences, then match the invitations to the responses.

Answers
1 Would you like to + **d** invitation
2 Shall I + **c** nice
3 Would you like + **b** rather
4 Would you like me to + **a** kind

3 Students write the number or letter of the phrase next to the function.

Watch out! Point out that we use *Would you like me to …?* to offer to do something for the other person. Make sure students don't say *Would you like that I …?*

Answers
a 1   b 2, 3, & 4   c a, c   d b, d

Pronunciation
Explain that flat intonation can sound ungracious with social phrases like these. Ask students to listen to the models on the recording carefully and then drill the phrases chorally and individually.

4 Give the students a few minutes to read the situations. Check understanding of vocabulary and proper names. In pairs, students take turns to make appropriate offers and invitations, and either accept or decline.

Watch out!
Madame Butterfly = opera by Puccini
Picasso = 20th century Spanish painter

Alternative
Student B in each pair tosses a coin. If it is heads, they accept the invitation or offer. If tails, they decline.

» If students need more practice, go to **Practice file 11** on page 122 of the **Student's Book**.

5 NB this activity will need to be adapted if all your students come from the same company or are pre-work (see *Pre-work learners* below). Give students a few minutes to think of six ideas for entertaining a guest either within their company or in their home town. Ask them to study the *Key expressions*. Then in pairs students 'visit' each others' companies and invite / offer and accept / decline.

Pre-work learners / Alternative
If your students are all from the same company: ask them to think of six ideas for looking after and entertaining a guest to their company. Then they take turns at being a guest from a foreign company, and the activity proceeds as above.
Pre-work: same as above, but the guest is visiting their place of study. Or they could imagine they work for a company in their home town, and proceed as above.

Feedback focus
Focus on correct use and pronunciation of the social language from this section, paying particular attention to intonation.

ⓘ Refer students to the **Interactive Workbook Email** and **Phrasebank** sections for further study and to the **Exercises and Tests** for revision.

Case study

Background
Corporate hospitality at football matches and so on has had a mixed press. On the one hand, real fans are resentful that tickets for big sporting occasions go to people who are not really interested in the event (and often don't watch it anyway). Players also complain that the corporate guests are not so enthusiastic or vocal in their support for the teams, which spoils the atmosphere. On the other hand, it is an excellent source of income for the clubs who might otherwise have to raise ticket prices for the ordinary fan.

From the host's point of view, the success of the event can depend on the quality of the entertainment and also of the standard of service provided by the company used for the entertainment and catering. This is the theme of this *Case study*.

Students study a scenario where a company has encountered problems with a previous corporate entertainment event and must decide on its future programme.

As a lead-in, ask the students what the title *A hospitality disaster* could mean, and what might have gone wrong.

Students then read the text and answer the questions.

Discussion

The questions can be discussed in open class, or in small groups.

Watch out! You might need to pre-teach the following.
sue = take somebody to court to get back money you have lost

> **Answers**
> 1 Various things went wrong with the arrangements, especially the catering.
> 2 (Suggested) They could have checked more at each stage of the preparation / appointed one of their own staff to check and liaise with the hospitality company.
> 3 (Possible) Bad weather / An accident / Transport problems / Event is cancelled / Poor service

Task

1 Explain to the students that they are in charge of arranging the next hospitality event for SFO. Put the students into four groups, A, B, C, and D. Each group reads a different File (21, 46, 29, and 58).

Watch out! Possibly problematic vocabulary items in Files
File 21:
Romeo and Juliet trail = a walk around the sights in Verona connected with Romeo and Juliet
Roman amphitheatre = open-air Roman theatre where operas are held in the summer
File 29:
exquisite = excellent, perfect
spa = area of the castle where you take health cures / relax in a sauna, etc.
vineyard = place where grapes are grown and wine is made
File 58:
MotoGP = international motorcycle race
marquee = large tent
pit lane = area where repairs are made, motorcycles fill up with petrol, change tyres, etc.

2 Each group discusses potential problems with their event, and how these problems could be avoided. Spend some time revising the first conditional to help them with the discussion. You may need to feed in ideas (see *Answers* below).

> **Possible answers**
> **File 21:**
> Hotel could be over-booked – check with hotel a week before / have back-up hotel ready
> Food at dinner not very good – ask to check menu and food the day before
> Opera is rained off – organize back-up – evening in traditional Italian 'trattoria'
> **File 46:**
> Guests not able to build boat – have an expert on hand to help
> Some participants cannot swim – send out questionnaire beforehand / organize place to watch from + free drink
> Food or service at barbecue not very good – ask to check menu and food the day before
> **File 29:**
> Transport doesn't arrive / is late – check with transport company two days before / have back-up transport available if needed
> Guests not interested in golf or spa facilities – have back-up trip available
> Guests don't like champagne – ask vineyard to provide other options
> **File 58:**
> Food and service not very good – ask to check menu and food the day before
> Marquee not situated where stated – send somebody to check beforehand
> Guests not interested in GP – have back-up activity arranged – visit to local garden / stately home?

3 Make new groups with students from each of the old groups. Each student presents their event, explaining potential problems and possible solutions. Students should ask each other questions using first conditionals, e.g:
  What will you do if it rains?
Each group decides which event to arrange.

One-to-one

Your student should read two of the Files, and come up with possible problems and solutions. You describe the other two Files, and the student should ask you about problems using the first conditional as above. Then together you discuss which event to choose.

» Unit 11 **Progress test** and **Speaking test**, pages 108–109.

12 | Performance

Unit content

By the end of this unit, students will be able to
- talk about performance
- talk about present and past performance using the present perfect
- say large numbers and approximate numbers
- describe trends.

Context

Company performance is a key part of business life. Traditional measures of a company's performance include profits, sales, and (in the case of a public company) the share price. However, these in themselves are no longer perceived as sufficient. Even the most successful companies need to address the field of corporate responsibility, so that a brand leader like Coca-Cola, in its annual report, not only talks about revenues and sales, but also addresses the issue of health and obesity, and talks of the company's involvement with health education programmes. Environmental performance, as we have seen in previous units, is another area where many companies have become acutely aware: for example, Ford make much on their website of the fact that their plant in Dagenham, UK, won an award for environmental performance and innovation. These factors, rather than being a cost, have become a potential asset.

In this unit, students will discuss and learn key vocabulary to do with evaluating performance. Connected with this is the question of how we *describe* performance, and, in particular, changes in performance, through statistics and graphs. The world of business is one where numbers and trends are minutely studied, and some language for describing these, both precisely and approximately, is presented here. The unit ends with a decision-making game which enables them to put into practice the language of the unit.

Starting point

Allow the students time to consider their responses to the questions. Then discuss in open class.

Possible answers
2 a state of the economy / wealth of the population / crime statistics / contentment of the people / number of people emigrating / prison population / press comment
  b number of goods sold / annual evaluation according to established criteria / popularity amongst staff / customer feedback / employee's own feedback / subjective view of his / her line managers

Working with words

1 Pre-teach *socially responsible*. Ask students for names of socially responsible companies. You could use this to review the vocabulary from Unit 10 on the environment. Students discuss the statements in pairs, then feed back briefly to the class.

Watch out! You may wish to pre-teach the following.
ethnic minorities = minority national or racial groups in a country
disabled = lacking physical or mental abilities

Answers
According to the text:
1 False – the text talks of 'every investor'
2 True
3 True
4 True
5 False – 46% believe this

2 Students go back to the text and complete the sentences with the words and phrases in bold.

Answers
1 diversity of its workforce
2 socially responsible
3 perform well
4 reputation
5 manages its costs
6 safety record
7 achieves its sales targets
8 environmental performance

Pronunciation
Drill the word stress:
ma̱nages, perfo̱rms, reputa̱tion, socially respo̱nsible, environme̱ntal perfo̱rmance, dive̱rsity.

3 Students should be paired with a partner from a different company if possible. They discuss the relative importance of the factors in **2**.

63

Pre-work learners

Students could discuss a company that they know well. An alternative would be for them to research a company out of class, find the answers to the question in **3**, and bring their research back to class.

4 54▷ Students listen and say which of the factors in **2** is being evaluated. As this activity practises listening for gist, don't pre-teach vocabulary at this point.

> **Answers**
> 1 diversity
> 2 safety record
> 3 shares performing well
> 4 environmental performance
> 5 managing costs

5 54▷ Students complete the sentences and then listen and check.

> **Answers**
> 1 disappointing
> 2 encouraging
> 3 excellent
> 4 poor
> 5 satisfactory

Pronunciation

Drill the word stress:
disappointing, encouraging, excellent, satisfactory.

6 Students match the adjectives in **5** to the definitions.

> **Answers**
> 1 satisfactory
> 2 encouraging
> 3 disappointing
> 4 excellent
> 5 poor

Extra activity

Students draw a line across the page and write the adjectives along the line from 'good' on the left to 'bad' on the right (answers: *excellent > encouraging > satisfactory > disappointing > poor*). What other adjectives could they add? (Possible answers: *outstanding, brilliant, good, fair, adequate, average, bad, terrible, awful.*)

Tip Refer students to the *Tip* about *disappointed / encouraged* or *disappointing / encouraged*.

Extension

Ask students if they know any similar pairs of words. (Possible answers: *frightened / frightening, excited / exciting, bored / boring, interested / interesting, tired / tiring, depressed / depressing, amazed / amazing, embarrassed / embarrassing*.) Ask students to write sentences to show their meaning.

» If students need more practice, go to **Practice file 12** on page 124 of the **Student's Book**.

7 Students will need some thinking time before they start speaking. They choose three of the topics and tell their partner about performance using the words in **5**.

ⓘ Refer students to the **Interactive Workbook Glossary** for further study.

Language at work

1 55▷ Students listen and answer the questions.

> **Answers**
> 1 Dubai   2 Lionel in 2004, Raul three years ago

2 55▷ Students listen again and underline the correct form.

Watch out! You might need to remind students of the terminology *past simple* and *present perfect*.

> **Answers**
> 1 opened
> 2 had
> 3 has gone up
> 4 've been
> 5 moved

3 Students look at the sentences again and complete the rules. If they are struggling, you can tell them that the choice in 1 and 2 is between the two tenses, and in 3 and 4 between *for* and *since*.

> **Answers**
> 1 past simple – Example: We opened our first sales office in 2004.
> 2 present perfect – Example: I have been in Dubai for three years now.
> 3 for – Example: I have been in Dubai for three years now./ We had disappointing results for the first two years.
> 4 since – Example: Since 2006, our market share has gone up …

Extension

If the students are having problems with *for / since*, read out the following list of time expressions and ask them to put up their left hand if they would use *for* and their right if they would use *since*:

2006, ten minutes, the day before yesterday, ten o'clock this morning, an hour, the end of last year, three days, twenty years

Answers
for: ten minutes, an hour, three days, twenty years
since: 2006, the day before yesterday, ten o'clock this morning, the end of last year

---

Then ask the students to choose five of the expressions and write true sentences in the present perfect using them.

4 Students work in pairs, and make sentences using the information in the table. They may need to consult the audio script on page 156 of the Student's Book.

Watch out! Some students may want to use the present perfect continuous when they see the verb *working* and *going up* in the table (e.g. *Its market share has been going up since 2006*). Accept these sentences if they are correct.

> **Possible answers**
> Lionel's company has had a sales office in Dubai since 2004.
> Its market share started going up in 2006.
> Lionel's company has had more encouraging results since 2006.
> Raul has lived in Dubai for three years.
> Raul's family arrived in Dubai last year.
> Raul's family has lived in Dubai for a year.

5 Start by asking students what they know about Dubai. Pre-teach *diversify*. Students read the information about Dubai and answer the questions. Weaker students could use a dictionary for this.

Watch out! You may need to pre-teach the following.
revenue = money earned (in this case, from oil)
aim = objective
average = typical amount

> **Answers**
> 1 It is trying to diversify its economy away from oil.
> 2 Yes, it has. It has reached its GDP target early, and now only 3% of the GDP comes from oil.

6 Ask students to read the *Tip* before they do this exercise. They then ask and answer the questions. As this is the first time they have used the question form of the present perfect, students may need a model on the board:
How long + has / have + subject + past participle?

Pronunciation

Make sure students pronounce *has / have* with a weak form /həz/ /həv/.

> **Answers**
> 2 How long has Dubai invested in services? Since the early 1990s.
> 3 When did the economy begin to grow very quickly? In 2000.
> 4 How long did it grow at 13.4% a year? For five years. / From 2000 to 2005.
> 5 How long has GDP been over $30 billion? Since 2005.
> 6 How long has the 'Dubai Strategic Plan' been in operation? Since 2007. / For X years (depending on date now).

Feedback focus

Focus on the correct grammar of the questions and the pronunciation of *has / have*. Students may need reminding about the formation of past simple questions.

» If students need more practice, go to **Practice file 12** on page 125 of the **Student's Book**.

7 Students work in pairs, and use questions with *How long?* and *When?* with the appropriate tense to find out things they have in common. Model the dialogues first: ask a student: *How long have you been in this room?* The student answers (for example): *Since 11 a.m*. You reply: *Me too! We have one thing in common*. Students read through the list and formulate questions in their heads. Then they ask and answer questions.

Feedback focus

To give them more practice with the two tenses, ask students to report back to class using *both,* e.g.
We have both worked for KME for two years.
We both lived in our last flat for more than five years.

Pre-work learners

Add these questions to the list:
- *be in your present class?*
- *finish your last school?*
- *have your present computer?*
- *start learning English?*

Unit 12 Performance

65

Practically speaking

1 56▷ A fun lead-in could be to ask students if they know the five different ways to say the number 0 in English. (Answer: *zero, nought, 'O', nil* (as in football games *2–0 = two–nil*), *love* (in tennis). Explain that numbers are problematic in English. Students study the numbers for a few minutes and try to say them. (They will probably find this difficult.) Then they listen and check.

Watch out! In some languages, the comma and full stop fulfil the reverse functions to English, so students may think, for example, that *7,467* is a number between 7 and 8. Make sure students don't use the plural **four hundreds* or say **one point thirty-nine*. American English omits *and* between hundreds and tens. You could tell students that *zero* is always acceptable for the figure 0, especially in American English.

> **Answers**
> 1 one point three nine per cent
> 2 nought point oh three three
> 3 one hundred and two
> 4 seven thousand four hundred and sixty seven
> 5 nine hundred and six thousand five hundred and seventy
> We use a full stop for a decimal point (i.e. between whole numbers and decimal fractions) and a comma after millions and thousands (i.e. every three whole digits). We use 'nought' before the decimal point but 'oh' after it.

2 57▷ Students listen to the stock market report and answer the questions.

> **Answers**
> Nikkei – up   Dow Jones – down
> FTSE 100 – up   Nasdaq – down
> DAX – up

3 57▷ Students listen again and complete the table. You may wish to play the recording twice or even three times. Students should check their answers in pairs.

> **Answers**
> Nikkei up 2.84%
> FTSE 100 + 38.6
> DAX + 0.07%
> Dow Jones - 69.85
> Nasdaq value 2316.91

4 Students use the table to practise saying the figures. One student speaks, the other listens and corrects.

Extra activity

Information gap. Type out a similar table, but with different figures. Make two copies. On copy A, white out about six of the figures. On copy B, white out a different six. Make photocopies so that half the students have A and half B. Students work in A / B pairs, and, without seeing their partner's sheet, must complete the table by asking about their missing figures. At the end, they put both sheets on the desk and check answers. This promotes accurate saying of the figures, and listening for numbers.

5 Students study the language of approximation. Check meaning using the *Tip* and pronunciation, especially of *roughly*. Students match them with figures from the table. NB two of the figures are amongst the answers to **3**.

> **Answers**
> 1 377.91   4 5.17
> 2 5932.20   5 38.6
> 3 69.85

6 Students say the figures using the approximations.

> **Possible answers**
> Nearly / just under / roughly / around $900
> Roughly / around / just over 7,000
> Nearly / just under / around / roughly 50%
> Just over €141

Business communication

1 58▷ Teach / elicit the word *trend*. Students describe the graph using their own words to start with. You could teach *horizontal / vertical axis*. Students speculate as to which line represents which country. They listen and check.

> **Answers**
> 1 USA   3 Japan
> 2 Germany   4 China

2 Students could use a dictionary for this exercise.

> **Answers**
> **Upward:** rise, grow, increase
> **Downward:** decrease, drop, fall, decline
> **No change:** remain stable

3 Students ask and answer about the graph in pairs.

Watch out! For this activity, students will need a few phrases to describe dates:
in the nineties, in the noughties, since (2000), between (1997) and (1999), from (1997) to (1999), at the start / end of the (nineties). You could also teach *will probably* + verb for the future.

4 58▷ Students compare the sentences to the graph, and say which countries are being described. They then listen again and check.

Answers	
1 Germany	3 USA
2 Germany	

5 Students study the use of the prepositions in **4** and complete the description.

> **Answers**
> Our sales went up **by** 500 units, **from** 2,500 in October **to** 3,000 in November. They stayed **at** 3,000 units in December.

» If students need more practice, go to **Practice file 12** on page 124 of the **Student's Book**.

6 Working in pairs, each student studies a different File. Explain that they have the same graph, but have missing information that only their partner can supply. Students must describe their graph using the language from this section, and their partner must mark in the sales of the missing company on their graph. Make sure they don't simply describe each month's sales individually, but actually use the verbs in **2** and the prepositions in **5** to describe trends. Students with File 22 should start. At the end, students compare graphs to check answers.

Watch out! Check students know the past simple of the irregular verbs in **2**: *rose, grew, fell*.

Feedback focus
Focus on correct use of the language from this section.

7 Students may have to find the graph before class or for homework. If this is not possible, and students have no knowledge of their company's / country's performance, ask them to draw a fictional graph (for example, a company's profits 1995–2012) and give it to another student to describe. Students study the *Key expressions* before they start.

Alternative
Each student brings in a graph they have found (e.g. on the Internet). Shuffle the graphs, and redistribute so that each student has a new graph. Students describe their new graph to the class, or write a description and post up on the wall next to the graph.

ⓘ Refer students to the **Interactive Workbook Email** and **Phrasebank** sections for further study and to the **Exercises and Tests** for revision.

Activity
This *Activity* is fairly self-explanatory, so allow students time to read the instructions. Explain that they will win or lose points according to their decisions, and the total number of points they gain will show their company performance, both in terms of sales and profits, but also in social responsibility.

When the students start the activity, make sure that one person in each group is keeping a record of their score (File 24 gives a score for each answer). Check that the students are taking time to discuss each option before moving to the next.

At the end, each group calculates their final score, and discloses it to the class.

Feedback focus
Part of your role during this activity may be helping with vocabulary. However, you should also monitor language work, and bring any common mistakes (especially relating to the language of this unit) to the students' attention at the end.

» Unit 12 **Progress test** and **Speaking test**, pages 110–111.

13 Future trends

Unit content

By the end of this unit, students will be able to
- talk about global issues
- make predictions
- respond to ideas
- predict future trends in the workplace.

Context

The intersection between global issues and business practice is likely to become a major factor in future decision making. In the past, the world of business has been accused of 'hiding their head in the sand' when it comes to global issues, but this may not be possible in the future, especially if precious resources start to run out. The impact of, say, oil running short will have a massive impact on all areas of everyday life, including business. This in turn will have knock-on effects on business practices. If petrol becomes so expensive that we cannot use cars to get to work, companies will have to invent new solutions such as increased teleworking. With technological developments happening faster, it may be that technology (and especially advances in computing / telecommunications) provides (part of) the answer. But the ability of the workforce to be flexible, and change behaviours quickly in response to a new world, will also be vital.

Some students will also see an ethical side to global issues. For example, on an everyday level, is it right for an office or school to have a water cooler that consumes electricity to cool the water, and plastic for the cups? At a higher level, is it ethical to adopt industrial processes which use a lot of raw materials? Companies that can show they are addressing these concerns may do better with the 'ethical consumer' and hence also improve the bottom line.

In this unit, students will talk about global issues, before moving on to look at the language of making predictions, in both a general and a business context. They will also discuss future trends in the workplace. The *Case study* deals with a specific case of updating a company in order to meet future demands.

Starting point

If your context allows, you could start by taking in the day's English-language newspapers, or set up a projector so that students can view a news website like www.bbc.co.uk or www.cnn.com. Ask students to browse and make a list of three or four current global issues. Students answer the questions in small groups. Monitor and supply vocabulary as necessary.

Pre-work learners

For question 3, students could imagine the effect of the issues on a local company, or one with which they are familiar.

Working with words

1 Ask what the *global oil crisis* is. (Answer: when the need in the world for oil is greater than the supply.) Ask students when they think this will happen. Then they read the text quickly and answer the question.

> **Answer**
> 2015

2 Students read the text more slowly and answer the questions in pairs or groups. When feeding back, ask the students to say where in the text they found the answers.

> **Answers**
> 1 to give us food, warmth, chemicals, medicine, and clothing
> 2 population growth and rapid economic development of countries like China and India
> 3 investing millions in renewable energy

Watch out! You may wish to pre-teach the following.
run out = come to an end (though this appears in **6** below)
exceed = become greater than
due to = because of
be upon us = arrive (suddenly)

Dictionary skills

Word building: students use dictionaries to find the nouns or verbs from these words in the text (answers in brackets).
  warmth (warm), mobility (mobile), supply (supply), predict (prediction), growth (grow), development (develop), forecast (forecast), invest (investment), solution (solve)

3 Students go back to the text and match the words in bold to the definitions.

Answers
1 renewable energy
2 global demand
3 economic development
4 energy crisis
5 population growth
6 oil shortage
7 world supply

Pronunciation
Make sure the students pronounce the phrases with the correct stress.
re*new*able *en*ergy, *glob*al dem*and*, eco*nom*ic de*vel*opment, *en*ergy *cri*sis, popu*la*tion *growth*, *oil short*age, *world sup*ply

Extension
Ask students to match these seven words to the second part of the phrases in **3**: *excess, financial, industrial, limited, nuclear, professional, staff*. (Answers: *excess demand, financial crisis, industrial growth, limited supply, nuclear energy, professional development, staff shortage*). Other answers may be possible.

4 Students test each other on the phrases. A variation could be for students to say the second word in the phrase, and their partner says the first.

5 59▷ Ask students to read through the five effects and check vocabulary. Then play the listening once and ask students to order the effects.

Answers
The effects are heard in this order: d, e, b, c, a

6 59▷ Students listen again and complete the sentences.

Answers
1 estimate
2 run out
3 forecast
4 improve
5 deteriorate

7 Students replace the word in bold with one of the verbs from **6**.

Answers
1 estimate
2 deteriorate
3 runs out
4 improve
5 forecast

» If students need more practice, go to **Practice file 13** on page 126 of the **Student's Book**.

8 Explain that the aim of the activity is to practise the verbs in **6**. Students should choose three issues and write one or two sentences for each, using a different verb in each case.

9 Students discuss the questions in pairs. Make sure you give some opportunity to discuss the questions in open class too.

Possible answers
Poverty – we could develop GM crops to feed the poor. We could force rich countries to give more to poor countries.
The energy crisis – we could pass laws forcing people to use public transport / restricting families to one car each / make cars smaller.
Population growth – we could pass laws restricting the number of children to one per couple.
Climate change – we could insist on a certain level of carbon emission reduction / spend more on educating children to the dangers / pass laws insisting on cleaner / greener factories, etc.
Sex equality – we could enforce more stringently existing equality laws / pass new laws making quotas for women in management, etc.
Racism – we could conduct anti-racist campaigns in schools and companies / discipline employees guilty of racist behaviour.

Alternative
Students debate which of the issues is the most important for the future of humanity.

i Refer students to the **Interactive Workbook Glossary** for further study.

Language at work
1 Write the title of the text on the board, and check the students understand what it means. In order to guide the students' discussion, you may wish to give them the four sub-headings from the text before they start talking. Students discuss the question in pairs and then feed back to open class. They then read the text and decide if the changes in the text are similar to the ones they suggested.

2 Students choose the correct answer and then check with the text.

Watch out! You might wish to pre-teach the following.
restructure = change the structure of something
workforce = people who work for a company
flexibility = capacity to change behaviour at short notice
leisure activities = activities you normally do outside work

Answers
1 may
2 might not
3 will
4 won't

Unit 13 | Future trends

69

3 Students complete the rules.

> **Answers**
> 1 will Example: no 3
> 2 may / might Example: no 1
> 3 may not / might not Example: no 2
> 4 won't Example: no 4

Tip Refer students to the *Tip* and check understanding of the language point. Practise the pronunciation of *won't* and make sure they can distinguish it from *want*.

4 60▷ Ask students to read the table carefully before they listen – they may be able to predict some of the answers. Students listen and tick the correct column.

Watch out! You might wish to pre-teach the following.
self-managed = managing yourself, without a boss

> **Answers (4 and 5)**
> The working population **will** be older.
> There **won't** be many management positions.
> Colleagues **might not** see each other often.
> Most people **will** work from home.
> There **won't** be a lot of offices in office buildings.
> Office buildings **might** contain a gym.
> Employees **may not** stay with the same company.
> Employers **will** offer better conditions.
> Employees **may** take career breaks.

5 This is a check for **4**. Students make sentences using their answers to **4**.

> **Answers**
> See **4**.

Feedback focus

Focus on the use of the modal verbs. You could point out that *might not* is contracted to *mightn't* but that *may not* is never contracted.

» If students need more practice, go to **Practice file 13** on page 127 of the **Student's Book**.

6 In pairs, students make predictions about their own jobs using the modal verbs in **3**.

Pre-work learners

You could give each student a 'job' and ask them to do the activity as if they did that job. Alternatively, you could ask them to make predictions about their place of learning / local or national economy / a company they know well.

Practically speaking

1 Start by making a suggestion to which the students might respond positively (*Why don't we all go out for a pizza tonight?*) and wait for reactions. Do the same with *I think I ought to give this class more homework*. Ask what the difference was in their reactions and elicit *positive* and *negative*. Then ask them to order the responses.

> **Answers**
> The correct order is d – a – c – e – b.

2 61▷ Pre-teach *staff turnover*. Ask the students to read the five suggestions and give their opinion of them. Students listen and match the suggestions to the responses in **1**.

> **Answers**
> 1 c   2 e   3 a   4 b   5 d

Pronunciation

Students should also imitate the intonation used by the speakers in the conversation. A fun extra activity is to ask them to pronounce the sound *Mmm* as if they were responding (a) positively (b) negatively (you will need to model this for them). English speakers often use this sound with the appropriate intonation to respond to ideas.

3 Revise or teach a few phrases for making suggestions (perhaps by playing the conversation again and asking students to write down the phrases they heard), e.g. *I think we should …, How / What about + -ing?, Why don't we …?, We could …*. Give students a few minutes to think of a few ideas. In pairs, they make suggestions and respond with the phrases in **1**.

Feedback focus

Focus on the stress and intonation of the responses.

Dictionary skills

Idioms: put students in groups of three. Each group looks up one or two verbs from the list. From the section of the entry marked 'idioms', they should note down one or two useful idioms containing their word and then present their idioms to the class.
Possible verbs from this unit: *offer, give, hold, stop, stay, work, think, make, grow*.
(NB before you do this activity, check (1) students have a good dictionary with a range of idioms (2) the idiom section is clearly marked.)

Business communication

1 Introduce the topic of *teleworking*. Students ask and answer the questions in pairs.

Answers
1 working at home, but remaining in contact with your work by phone / email, etc.
2 **Possible answers:**
Advantages: employees don't waste time commuting; they can be more flexible and comfortable in their work arrangements; they can get a job even if they live somewhere remote; the company doesn't need to provide so much workspace and car parking; it can increase productivity.
Disadvantages: employees can feel isolated; it is more difficult to meet clients; it is more difficult to build a 'team'; colleagues can be jealous; how can the employer monitor performance?

2 62▷ Students listen and compare their list of advantages from **1** with the items they hear.

3 62▷ Students listen again and put the sentences in order.

Answers
The correct order is g – c – f – h – d – a – e – b.

4 Students read the sentences in **3** again, and complete the table.

Answers
Asking for predictions: Do you think … will …? / Is … likely to …?
Making predictions: It probably won't … / … is unlikely to …
Expressing hope: Hopefully … will / won't … / I hope … will …

Watch out! You may need to point out the grammar of *likely / unlikely: be + likely / unlikely + to + verb*. If you feel students need more practice, ask them to write two or three true sentences about themselves e.g. *I am unlikely to get a new job in the near future*.

5 Give students a few minutes to read through the ideas. Weaker students could write down a few sentences including the phrases in **4**. Students ask and answer using the ideas.

Feedback focus

Focus on use of the target language and especially the correct use of *likely / unlikely*.

» If students need more practice, go to **Practice file 13** on page 126 of the **Student's Book**.

6 Make sure the students understand that the objective of this activity is to practise the language from this section. (A variation would be to award points to students who use the phrases.) Ask them to read *Key expressions*. Give them plenty of time to think about the scenario and come up with ideas. Ask the class if any students use videoconferencing at the moment, and what its advantages and drawbacks are. Students pretend to work for the same company and discuss the proposal from Head Office.

Feedback focus

Make a note of common errors and bring them to the attention of the class.

One-to-one

Make sure the student has plenty of opportunity to ask questions using the phrases.

ⓘ Refer students to the **Interactive Workbook Email** and **Phrasebank** sections for further study and to the **Exercises and Tests** for revision.

Unit 13 Future trends

Case study

Background

This *Case study* presents a situation where a corporation (in this case, BMW) has made major structural changes to a company which it has acquired, and which suffers from problems of different kinds. In the *Task,* it then asks the students to do the same for an imaginary company. In an era of very quick change, it demonstrates how an ailing company can quite quickly be turned around given the necessary 'surgery' (NB the Mini plant in Oxford is a major success story – it produced its millionth car for export in July 2008.)

As a lead-in, ask the students if they have ever worked for a company during a time of major changes. What happened and why? If not, ask them to think of changes they would make to their present company (if any).

Students then read the text about BMW at Cowley.

Watch out! You may wish to pre-teach the following.
take over = get control of (a company)

Discussion

The questions can be discussed in open class, or in small groups. Once they have had plenty of time to discuss, ask them to read File 25 on page 140 of the Student's Book.

> **Answers**
> 1 low productivity, outdated machinery, expensive and impractical production, poor relations between management and workforce, the main brand could not meet the needs of the customer.
> 2/3 Students' own answers

Watch out! Possibly problematic vocabulary items in File 25: *shift* = one of the periods that the working day is divided into, e.g. the night shift.

Task

1 Ask students to read the instructions and explain the situation to you. Put students into pairs, and ask them to read File 26 together. Students discuss the company in pairs and suggest changes. Make sure they come up with plenty of ideas, even very unconventional ones – they can always discard them later. Stress they can (but do not have to) adopt ideas from the BMW scenario.

2 Each pair joins with another pair to make groups of four.

3 They choose the six best ideas from the two pairs.

One-to-one

Omit the pair and groupwork. The student reads File 26, and you and he / she discuss the options as a pair.

Watch out! You may want to teach some possibly problematic vocabulary items in File 26.
rundown = in bad condition
outskirts = areas around the edge of a town
fined = had to pay money as a punishment for breaking the law

» Unit 13 **Progress test** and **Speaking test**, pages 112–113.

14 | Time

Unit content

By the end of this unit, students will be able to
- talk about managing time
- speculate and discuss consequences using conditional sentences
- talk about time
- negotiate conditions.

Context

Time management is a big issue in current business thinking, and large numbers of experts, companies, and websites have sprung up to help us with it. Some of these undoubtedly provide useful advice, especially on how to deal with modern technology, which although supposedly making our lives easier and quicker, often clogs them up with emails and texts. From the students' point of view, especially if they are pre-work learners, time management has an extra significance because it is useful for their study as well as their work.

There is also a cultural element. Some cultures, for example, approve of somebody who works long hours, whilst another will see them as inefficient and probably a time-waster. Also, traditionally (and perhaps stereotypically), we tend to divide cultures into those where time and punctuality are important and those where people are more relaxed about it. This divide has become more significant as business becomes global, and we can end up working with colleagues of any background.

The second area in this unit is negotiation. Different cultures negotiate differently, and it is not the case that the Western norm of working towards a compromise is necessarily accepted by all.

Both these topics should provide a good starting point for intercultural exchange if you have a suitable class. And in both areas, we could ask the question: does an individual person's attitude derive mainly from their culture, or simply from their own personality? This unit helps the students to explore these questions. They will also learn about negotiating, and practise what they have learnt throughout the unit in the *Case study* on scheduling and meeting deadlines.

Starting point

Give the students a few minutes to read the questions and consider their answers. They then discuss them in pairs or small groups. You may wish to teach the phrase *time management*.

Extension

If your students work with different nationalities, ask if they think different cultures have different attitudes to punctuality and time planning. Ask for their experiences in this area.

Working with words

1 Write *multitasking* on the board and elicit the meaning. Ask: *Do you have to multitask in your job?* Then ask students to answer and then discuss the questions in pairs.

2 Students read the text and find the answers to the questions in **1**.

Answers
1 b   2 b   3 a

Watch out! You may wish to pre-teach the following.
workplace-organizer expert = an expert who deals with the organization of the workplace

3 Students choose the correct alternative using the text to help them.

Answers
1 waste   3 allow
2 plan   4 enough, deadline

4 Students write sentences using the phrases they did not use in **2**. Stronger students can do this orally. Tell students they can change the grammatical form if they want.

Possible answers
1 If you save time, you use your time well.
2 I usually spend some time every day talking to colleagues.
3 I was on time for the meeting.

Watch out! You may wish to point out some grammatical features of the phrases.
waste / save time + verb-*ing*
allow time / have enough time + *to* + verb

5 Pre-teach the useful construction *save time by* + -*ing* (which also comes up in **6**). Give students a few minutes to think of some ideas. (You could write key words on the board to help students who do not have experience of meetings.) Encourage use of the phrases in **3**.

Possible answers
See **6**

73

6 Students complete the advice with suitable words and phrases.

> **Answers**
> 1 Plan
> 2 Save
> 3 on time
> 4 Spend
> 5 deadline
> 6 waste, allow
> 7 enough time

Watch out! You may wish to point out or elicit the difference between *on time* and *in time*:
on time = punctual, arriving at the scheduled time
in time = early enough.

Tip Refer students to the *Tip* about *enough*. Point out that *enough* often follows an adjective in a negative sentence, as in the example. Ask them to make a few sentences with nouns and adjectives for practice.

Extra activity

Divide the class into two teams. Read out the nouns and adjectives below one by one and the first team to say a correct sentence with the word and *enough* wins a point. You could give extra points for particularly humorous or imaginative ones.
time, good, quick, money, customers, efficient, space, homework, big

» If students need more practice, go to **Practice file 14** on page 128 of the **Student's Book.**

7 If possible, put students into pairs of different jobs. You could structure the discussion by asking students to make a two-column table with problems on the left, and their solutions on the right. Give time to discuss their ideas in open class.

Pre-work learners

You may need to change the focus of this discussion slightly – ask students to concentrate on school / college deadlines, how they organize study time and relaxation periods during their week, whether they study / do assignments at the same time each week, whether they answer their mobile when writing an assignment, etc. You could use this activity to recap on good study strategies.

ⓘ Refer students to the **Interactive Workbook Glossary** for further study.

Language at work

1 63▷ Elicit the situation from the students by asking them to look at the photo and speculate. They listen and answer the questions.

> **Answers**
> 1 Yes
> 2 Only for a short period

2 63▷ Students listen again and underline the words they hear.

Watch out! You may wish to pre-teach the following.
pace = speed (though this is guessable from the context)

> **Answers**
> 1 I'd, lived
> 2 would, offered
> 3 was, might
> 4 wanted, wouldn't

3 You may wish to recap the first conditional from Unit 11. Students read the two sentences and complete the rules.

Watch out! Students may be confused by the fact that we use the past simple after *if* to talk about the future. You could point out that the past tense is used in English to show distance of some kind – distance in time (as in talking about past) or distance of probability as in the second conditional.

> **Answers**
> 1 first conditional
> 2 second conditional
> 3 past simple, base form of verb

4 Students look back at the sentences in **2** and answer the question.

> **Answer**
> might

5 Students complete the sentences by applying the rules in **3**.

> **Answers**
> 1 you had, would you choose
> 2 would you feel, your boss asked
> 3 you could, would interest
> 4 there was, would you spend
> 5 Would you be, mobile phones didn't exist
> 6 didn't have, would it be
> NB *might* can replace *would* in all the sentences.

6 Students ask and answer the questions in **5**. Encourage the use of *might* where appropriate.

» If students need more practice, go to **Practice file 14** on page 129 of the **Student's Book.**

7 As a lead-in, ask students for a general overview of attitudes to time and punctuality in their country. Then write *clock time* and *event time* on the board, and ask students to say what they think the phrases mean. Students read the texts and answer the questions in pairs. When you discuss the questions, be prepared for some lively responses, as some students may object to a whole culture being stereotyped in this way.

Watch out! You might need to pre-teach the following.
dictate = influence strongly, decide

8 Students work in pairs. Student A reads File 27 and Student B File 48. Check understanding of vocabulary. For the task, ask them to read the examples carefully – make sure they understand that they need to construct questions in the second conditional from the information given. Also, that they should make a note of both their own, and their partner's answers. When they have completed the questionnaire, they should look at File 57 for the answers. Leave some time for a discussion at the end with the whole class.

Watch out! Possible vocabulary problems from the Files.
File 27:
quotation = statement of how much a piece of work will cost
File 48:
irritable = annoyed
checkout = place in a supermarket where you pay

Feedback focus
Focus on the correct construction of second conditional questions.

One-to-one
Play the part of Student B.

Practically speaking

1 64▷ As a lead-in, you could ask students if they are flexible about time and deadlines. Get some examples. Students listen to the two conversations, and answer the question.

> **Answer**
> Conversation 1: finish a report
> Conversation 2: send a quotation

2 64▷ Students listen again and match the phrases.

> **Answers**
> 1 g 2 f 3 e 4 b 5 a 6 d 7 c

3 Students study the phrases and answer the question. Then they order the phrases from most to least urgent. Make sure they realize they are working from today as Wednesday.

> **Answers**
> The non-specific phrases are: as soon as possible / when you have time
> The correct order is: right away – by Friday – on Monday – within a week – before the end of next week

Watch out! You may wish to give more information about meaning and use.
by = 'on or before' and is used with specific times or days / dates
on is used with a day or date
within = inside a period of time

4 Students use the prompts to ask for things.

> **Suggested answers**
> 2 Can you give me the report by 5 p.m?
> 3 Can you give me confirmation of the meeting by the end of the week?
> 4 I'd like the budget figures before the end of the year.
> 5 I need to see the new product right away.
> 6 Can we have a meeting on Thursday?

Feedback focus
Focus on the correct use of the time expressions.

Dictionary skills
Using dictionaries for grammar work: ask students to look up the following verbs (from this unit), and find out which verb patterns can follow each one (including prepositions). The answer may be in the grammar information given by the dictionary or in the examples.

1 waste time   4 propose
2 succeed   5 offer (v)
3 plan (v)   6 agree

Answers
1 + *-ing* / + *on* + *-ing*
2 + *in* + *-ing*
3 + *to* + verb / + *on* + *-ing*
4 + *to* + verb / + *-ing*
5 + *to* + verb
6 + *to* + verb / + *that* + subject + *should* / *would*, etc.

Business communication

1 65▷ Pre-teach *machine tool manufacturer*. Ask the students to read the instructions and speculate about what the problem and solutions might be. They listen and complete the information.

> **Answers**
> **Problem:** a lorry drivers' strike. Luca won't be able to deliver the order on time.
> **First solution:** sending the goods by train.
> **Disadvantage of first solution:** the order won't arrive in time for production.
> **Second solution:** train to the border, where a lorry from Hans-Peter's company will pick it up.
> **Who will pay?** Luca's company

Watch out! You may wish to point out the use of *basically* to introduce an explanation.

2 65▷ Students match the sentences halves. Then they listen again and check their answers.

> **Answers**
> 1 c 2 d 3 i 4 a 5 g 6 h 7 j 8 e 9 b 10 f

Pronunciation

Ask students to listen to the conversation again and mark the sentence stress on the sentences in **2**.

3 Students match the functions to the sentences. Once they have done that, give them plenty of opportunity to practise them.

> **Answers**
> 1 Sentences 1 and 2   4 Sentences 6 and 9
> 2 Sentences 3 and 5   5 Sentences 4 and 7
> 3 Sentence 8   6 Sentence 10

Extra activity

Give the class one word from a sentence in **2** as a prompt to elicit the sentences. Students must produce the sentences using the prompt word. Then they do the same in pairs.

4 Make sure the students have had a chance to practise the sentences in **2**. They study the situation in **4** and think of ways they could use the sentences in **2** in the new context. Weaker students could write their ideas down. Check vocabulary. Students work in pairs to negotiate according to the instructions.

Feedback focus

Focus on use of the sentences from **2**. Students may need to do the activity several times to increase their fluency with the new language. Bring to the students' attention any examples of over-aggressive intonation.

» If students need more practice, go to **Practice file 14** on page 128 of the **Student's Book**.

5 Students read the *Key expressions*. Check stress and intonation again. Then ask the students to work in pairs and read the relevant Files. Check vocabulary and that they understand the situation. Stress that the aim of the negotiation is to come to an agreement, not to have a fight! Then students negotiate using the expressions.

Feedback focus

Apart from focusing on the use of the target language, you should also find out from each pair (if possible) what their final deal was, as students will probably be interested in who was the 'best' negotiator.

ⓘ Refer students to the **Interactive Workbook Email** and **Phrasebank** sections for further study and to the **Exercises and Tests** for revision.

Case study

Background

This *Case study* develops the area of negotiation by focusing on the construction industry. Various high-profile cases have demonstrated how many such projects fail to meet their deadline (and are often over-budget as well), and the *Case study* starts with a very extreme example, the Ryugyong hotel in North Korea, still uncompleted after twenty years. (Students could be asked for similar examples from their own countries.)

The *Case study* then moves on to a fictional example, where the students are required to first plan and then negotiate a schedule for construction. As in real life, a number of factors must be taken into consideration, and the order in which the various elements must be completed is important. For this reason, students should read the Files with particular care.

Discussion

Start by asking students if they have experience of construction projects. Then ask them to read the text and discuss the questions.

Watch out! In order for students to understand the text in detail, you may need to pre-teach: *revolving* = going round and round.

> **Answers**
> 1 there have been problems with building methods and materials
> **2 and 3** Students' own answers

Task

Ask students to read the background information. Check the meaning of *subcontract*. Establish today's date, and that the site is about to be closed for one month.

1 Students study the chart carefully. Establish which company is supposed to do which work, according to the symbols.

2 In pairs, students read File 30. Make sure the students understand the information in detail, and in particular the restrictions on scheduling. They then discuss a possible new schedule.

3 Students work with a new partner. First they read their respective Files (23 and 50). Make sure they understand the objectives of each student in the negotiations. NB Students A will need their new schedule from **2**, and will need to explain it to Student B. The students negotiate a new schedule and new costings.

One-to-one

It is probably better for your student to be Student A (File 23) in the negotiation, as this provides more continuity from the previous discussion.

Feedback focus

As with the previous negotiations in this unit, make sure you feed back on both language issues and the results of the negotiation.

» Unit 14 **Progress test** and **Speaking test**, pages 114–115.

15 Training

Unit content

By the end of this unit, students will be able to
- talk about personal development and training
- give advice using modal verbs
- say thank you and respond
- show understanding and suggest solutions.

Context

Improvement – in the form of personal development and training – is a key issue in business today. Since the students will, by definition, be undertaking a training course of some kind, it should be an area of relevance to them. The modern member of staff changes job and company more frequently than in the past, and one path to finding better jobs and gaining promotion is through gaining extra skills. The companies that offer this are more likely to retain staff. Some companies may complain that they train the staff, who then leave. But the alternative is *not* training them – and then they will leave. Or, worse, they'll stay!

Professional development (i.e. the development of technical skills to do with the job) has always been seen as the responsibility of the employer, but increasingly *personal* development is too. This is linked with the need to motivate staff through setting and achieving goals, appraisals to check progress, and giving constructive feedback on performance. Many managers are not trained to do these tasks, which can cause problems.

These issues are explored in the unit, which also gives the students the language and tools to give advice, suggest solutions, and reassure colleagues in difficult situations. The *Case study* at the end of the unit allows students to think about and discuss one company's personal development programmes and to come up with ideas for improvement.

Starting point

Students should discuss the questions in pairs, and then briefly in open class. Try to pair students with different jobs if possible. Monitor carefully and provide vocabulary as required.

Pre-work learners

You could give students an invented job and ask them to discuss as if they did that job. Alternatively, they could apply the questions to their current situation, with *course* replacing *job* and *school / college* replacing *company*.

Extra activity

Students work in groups of three or four. They think of a job, and then write a list of the skills needed for that job. They read out the skills one by one, and other groups try to guess the job.

Working with words

1 Write *business coach* on the board. Elicit the meaning (answer: a person who helps you to work better in your job). You could ask what the benefits of one might be. Students read the text quickly and decide with a partner if they would like one.

2 Students read the article more carefully and answer the questions.

> **Answers**
> 1 £3,000
> 2 enrol with a business coach
> 3 a Yes b Yes c No d Yes e No
> 4 He spends less time at work, but the work he does helps the company more (*work on* = improve)

3 Students match the phrases in bold in the article to the meanings.

> **Answer**
> 1 take a step back   5 set goals
> 2 motivate   6 achieving goals
> 3 develop your skills   7 improve your promotion prospects
> 4 improve your performance 8 give feedback

Pronunciation

Ask the students to underline the main stress in each phrase.
take a <u>step</u> <u>back</u>, <u>mo</u>tivate, de<u>vel</u>op your <u>skills</u>, im<u>prove</u> your per<u>for</u>mance, <u>set</u> <u>goals</u>, a<u>chie</u>ving <u>goals</u>, im<u>prove</u> your pro<u>mo</u>tion <u>pros</u>pects, give <u>feed</u>back

4 Students complete the sentences with words and phrases from **3**. Then they ask and answer the questions.

> **Answers**
> 1 motivate
> 2 set any goals, achieve
> 3 give you feedback
> 4 improve your promotion prospects
> 5 take a step back
> 6 skills, develop
> 7 improve your performance

Watch out! You may need to pre teach *annual appraisal* (= yearly meeting between manager and employee to discuss their aims and progress at work).

Pre-work learners

Change the questions to:
1 What things _____ you to study hard?
2 At the start of this course / year, did you _____ any _____? What are you doing to try and _____ them?
3 How often does your teacher _____ you _____ on your performance?
4 Do you think training would be the best way to _____ a person's _____ _____? What other ways are there to move up in the company?
5 When is the best time for somebody to _____ a _____ _____ from their job?
6 What new _____ would you like to _____ in your personal or academic life?
7 Have you done any training courses recently to _____ your _____ at school? How have these courses helped you?

Feedback focus

Focus on the correct use and pronunciation of the phrases from **3**.

5 There is some overlap between the answers here, so spend a little time getting the students to discuss and justify their answers.

Watch out! Make sure students say *project* with the stress on the first syllable.

> **Answers**
> 1 Managing stress
> 2 Communication skills
> 3 Time management
> 4 Motivating employees
> 5 Project management

» If students need more practice, go to **Practice file 15** on page 130 of the **Student's Book.**

6 66▷ You could introduce this listening by asking in what situations managers meet with employees. Ask for some examples from their own businesses. How many of the meetings are accidental and how many planned? Students listen and match the conversations to the situations.

> **Answers**
> 1 b   2 c   3 a

7 66▷ Students listen again and identify what Scott is doing wrong. Then they look back of the list of courses in **4** and decide which courses he should take and why.

> **Answers**
> 1 **Extract 1:** because the goals Scott had set were not stated at the previous appraisal
> **Extract 2:** the meeting is not effective because Scott hadn't listened to his employees and hasn't told them what he wants to discuss (or maybe he decides on the spot)
> **Extract 3:** Scott has not finished a task because he has got distracted by other tasks.
> 2 (suggested):
>   1 Motivating employees (for better feedback and setting goals
>   2 Communication skills (for better listening and effective meetings)
>   3 Time management

8 Students think about which courses would be good for them, and why. They could write the reasons down.

9 Model the exchange first: say the reason and get the students to suggest a course. Then students take turns to do the same.

ⓘ Refer students to the **Interactive Workbook Glossary** for further study.

Language at work

1 If your class has a lot of work experience, you could ask them to exchange experiences of appraisals, and decide what makes a good or poor one. They read the advice as if the gaps are not there, and say if they agree or not. (NB some of the points are actually the opposite of what is advised in **2**.)

2 67▷ Students listen and compare the speaker's opinion with the students' opinions from **1**.

> **Answers**
> 1 No
> 2 No
> 3 Yes, especially if they are shy
> 4 No
> 5 Yes
> 6 Yes

Unit 15 | Training

79

3 67▷ Students listen again and complete the advice in **1** with the correct modal verb.

Watch out! You may find students will ask you for the meanings of the verbs at this point. Tell them you will study this in the next activity.

> **Answers**
> 1 shouldn't
> 2 mustn't
> 3 could
> 4 shouldn't
> 5 should
> 6 must

Pronunciation

Make sure the students do not pronounce the middle /t/ in *mustn't*.

4 Students complete the sentences.

> **Answers**
> 1 must
> 2 should
> 3 could
> 4 shouldn't
> 5 mustn't

Tip Refer students to the *Tip* about *have to* and *must*. You could tell them that in many cases it is possible to use either, and in any case they will not be misunderstood if they use the other verb. The question form is usually with *have to*: *Do you have to wear a uniform?*

Extension

You could extend the *Tip* to talking about the difference between *don't have to* and *mustn't,* where there is a clear distinction in meaning. *You don't have to do something* means it is not necessary but you can if you want. *You mustn't do something* means it is not allowed or strongly inadvisable.

5 The answers to this exercise are highly subjective and could provoke interesting discussion. Give the students time to read through the advice, and monitor for vocabulary problems. Don't let them discuss the ideas yet, as that is the focus of **6**.

6 Students discuss the ideas using the modal verbs.

Feedback focus

Focus on the students' correct use of the modals. Make sure they contract the negatives, and pronounce *mustn't* correctly. Use their reasons to check they have understood the concept of each modal.

7 Students read the profiles. Ask the students if they know anybody in a similar situation. Students discuss the questions in pairs. Make sure they use the modal verbs from **3** when they are discussing the question.

» If students need more practice, go to **Practice file 15** on page 131 of the **Student's Book.**

8 68▷ Students listen to the experts and compare their answers.

> **Answers**
> **Marek:**
> take a holiday with his wife and children
> take a step back
> work on his management skills
> take a course in time management and managing people
> hire a personal coach
> talk to his team
> set clear goals for them and make them responsible for meeting their own deadlines
> **Klaudia:**
> talk to her boss first
> ask what she can do to improve her promotion prospects
> speak to the CEO (but not before she has spoken to her boss)
> say she will leave if she can't get management experience with this company

9 Students ask their partners for advice on how to do the things listed. Tell them they should formulate the problem properly using the prompts e.g. *I don't feel motivated in my current job, and I need some advice on how to increase my motivation.* The other student listens and gives advice using the modal verbs. Encourage use of all five verbs from **3**.

One-to-one

Take the part of the person asking for advice so as to give your student maximum opportunity for practice of the modal verbs.

Feedback focus

Note down the best pieces of advice (in terms of both grammar and content) and write them on the board at the end. Ask for students' reactions.

Practically speaking

1 Explain to students that thanking somebody is not as straightforward as it seems! You must choose the right level of formality, depending on what the other person has done for you, and on the relationship between you.

Suggested answers
a Thanks. / Thanks a lot.
b Thank you. / Thank you very much.
c Thanks for that. / Thanks for your help.
d Many thanks. / That was kind of you.

2 69▷ Students listen and match the conversations to the situations in **1**.

Answers
1 d   2 a   3 c   4 b

3 69▷ Students listen again and do the tasks.

Answers
A:
It was very nice of you to **think of me.**
Thanks **very much**.
Thanks for **helping me**.
Thank you for **all your help and advice**.
B:
You're welcome.
That's OK.
Not at all.
No problem.

4 Students look back at **3** and decide which phrases are more informal.

Answers
Thanks **very much**.
Thanks for **helping me**.
That's OK.
No problem.

5 Students practise using the expressions in **3**.

6 Students practise with the new situations. Make sure they think about the formality.

Suggested answers
1 Thanks for doing that.
   No problem.
2 It was very nice of you to invite me.
   You're welcome. It was fun, wasn't it?
3 Thanks very much for helping me with that.
   That's OK.

Business communication

1 Students ask and answer the questions in pairs.

Answers
1 (possible) because they have a deadline / they are not good at managing their time / something unexpected came up during the day / they take on other people's work
2 Students' own answers

2 70▷ Make sure the students read the questions before they listen.

Answers
1 to finish the annual report
2 she has a meeting at her son's school
3 she is going to the theatre
4 she doesn't understand the new software she's using
5 (they say) they don't have the money for it
6 next Monday
7 when there's a deadline, work comes first

3 70▷ Students listen again and number the sentences as they hear them.

Answers
The correct order is 1 – 5 – 7 – 6 – 2 – 8 – 3 – 4.

4 Put the students into pairs. Ask them to read the relevant Files. They then take turns to describe their problem and show understanding respectively.

5 71▷ Briefly recap Marisa's problem from **2**. Ask students to work in pairs and discuss what she should do. (This is another chance to use the modal verbs from this unit.) Then students listen to Glen and answer the questions.

Answers
1 coming back to work after the meeting / coming in at the weekend / telling Tom she's going to work on Saturday
2 telling Tom she's going to work on Saturday

6 71▷ Students listen again and complete the suggestions and responses.

Answers
1 Perhaps you could   a can't do that
2 Have you thought of   b might be possible
3 Why don't you   c good idea

» If students need more practice, go to **Practice file 15** on page 130 of the **Student's Book**.

Unit 15 | Training

81

Feedback focus
Monitor for correct use of the expressions from **1**, including natural stress, rhythm, and polite intonation.

7 Students read the relevant Files and the *Key expressions*. Check the stress and intonation of the *Key expressions*. The students then take turns to explain the problem, suggest solutions, and respond.

ⓘ Refer students to the **Interactive Workbook Email** and **Phrasebank** sections for further study and to the **Exercises and Tests** for revision.

Case study

Background
This *Case study* focuses on personal development, an area of increasing interest to companies as they seek to add value to the employment experience – and retain staff. Companies vary considerably in the extent to which they are proactive in these programmes: some, as in the *Background* material here, see it as a major benefit for the personnel as it is perceived as improving performance and quality of work. Others, typified by the invented company in the *Task*, have neither the inclination nor the belief to instigate (and, more importantly, keep up) such programmes. In this *Case study*, the students are asked to study both types of company and suggest ways in which a company where the employees are dissatisfied in this area can improve.

Discussion
Start by writing the title of the text *Helping employees to succeed and grow* on the board. What do they understand by it? Is it a company's duty to do this? What might a company do to achieve this aim? Then ask students to read the text and answer the questions. Give some time for discussion in groups or open class.

Watch out! You may wish to pre-teach the following.
silicon = an element used in making computer chips
mentor = someone who helps you in your job, especially over a period of time
higher education = university-level education or equivalent
accredited = recognized or approved

> **Answers**
> **1** It can reduce performance, quality of work, and efficiency.
> **2 / 3** Students' own answers

Task
1 72▷ Students listen and take notes on the complaints made. Then they answer the question in pairs.

> **Answers**
> They need to:
> provide appropriate training courses e.g. in English language so that employees have opportunities for promotion (Speaker 1)
> advertise jobs internally so that employees have a good chance to make an application (1)
> carry out appraisals as they should do (2)
> give positive feedback as well as negative (2)
> provide opportunities for employees to find out about technical questions to do with their job, e.g. by talking to experts within the company (3)
> build teamwork (4)

2 Students work in pairs to come up with ideas for Lektra. Give them plenty of time for this.

> **Possible answers**
> put in place a structure for sending employees on training courses and / or provide online courses
> make sure it is easy for employees to apply for jobs within the company
> make sure appraisals are carried out
> managers should go on training courses in techniques for doing appraisals and / or time management
> a system should be organized to allow employees a certain amount of time per year to be mentored in technical aspects of their jobs by experts from within the company
> 'Employee of the Month' should be scrapped, to be replaced by bonuses for the whole team if targets are met
> team bonding should be encouraged by weekends away together e.g. paintballing or murder mystery weekends

3 Each pair presents their ideas, and together the class chooses three, voting if necessary.

One-to-one
Depending on the creativity and imagination of your student, you may need to prompt with ideas in **2**. Omit **3**.

 » Unit 15 **Progress test** and **Speaking test**, pages 116–117.

16 | Your career

Unit content

By the end of this unit, students will be able to
- talk about ambitions and careers
- revise tenses / grammar
- say goodbye
- give a personal presentation.

Context

Many, if not all, of the students in the class, will be thinking about their career, since attendance at a course of this kind implies a need to improve their prospects or train for future success. Of course, a person's career is often a mixture of the planned and the lucky. Some people drift into a job and find it to be all they were looking for; others spend years training to fulfill an ambition, only to find they have made a ghastly mistake. Most people are somewhere in the middle.

It is probably true to say that careers advice has become much more proactive and focused than in the past. Career paths are more carefully mapped out, and all kinds of psychological testing are used to find the client the ideal job. At the same time, there is a much stronger tendency to change careers midway, not necessarily because you feel you have made a wrong choice, but because people change over time, and what is important to you at 20 may no longer be so at 45. Another reason is that industries or occupations become obsolete and workers must be more flexible. This unit gives the students the chance to talk about ambitions and careers, and make a personal presentation.

As the last unit in the book, the unit also gives the students the opportunity to review some of the important grammatical points and, appropriately, to practise ways of saying goodbye.

Starting point

Allow the students time to think about the questions. They then discuss them in pairs and small groups (of mixed nationality if possible). Question 4 could be discussed as a class.

Working with words

1 Ask the students to look at the photo of Greg Mortensen and find out if they have heard of him or his book *Three cups of tea*. They could speculate as to what it might be about. Then they read the text and answer the question.

> **Answer**
> He was a trauma nurse. Now he raises money for charities and builds schools in South Asia.

Watch out! You may wish to pre-teach the following.
trauma nurse = a nurse who specializes in helping patients who have suffered a severe injury

2 Students read the text again slowly and answer the questions.

> **Answers**
> 1 About fifteen years ago when he was climbing in the Himalayas.
> 2 He wrote to celebrities. He collected pennies.
> 3 He spends six months every year building schools in South Asia. It is not stated what he does for the other six months.

3 Students match the words and phrases in bold to the definitions.

> **Answers**
> 1 gave up   5 made the decision
> 2 completed   6 concentrate on
> 3 career path   7 spent
> 4 changed direction

Watch out! Tell students that *give up* and *concentrate on* are both followed by the verb in the *-ing* form.

Extension

Point out that *give up* and *concentrate on* are both examples of multi-word verbs, i.e. a main verb and a particle. However, they differ in their grammar: *give up* is separable (you can put the object before the particle as in *He gave the house up* and, if the object is a pronoun, you must, as in *He gave it up*). *Concentrate on* is inseparable, and the object always comes after the particle – *concentrate on it*. Give students the following list of common multi-word verbs and ask them to find out from a good dictionary if they are separable (S) or inseparable (I): *take up* (S), *agree to* (I), *call off* (S), *turn down* (S), *look for* (I), *apply for* (I), *fill in* (S), *wait for* (I), *send back* (S), *complain about* (I). Then ask them to use the verbs in sentences.

4 Tell students that they may have to change the order or grammar of the sentence to accommodate the phrases in brackets.

> **Suggested answers**
> 2 She completed her studies in 1989.
> 3 He spent two years training in an architect's studio.
> 4 Her career path is to study medicine, go abroad for some work experience, do her exams, and qualify as a family doctor.
> 5 He gave up his job in the city and moved to the country.
> 6 He changed direction to become an actor.
> 7 She wants to concentrate on painting.

5 73▷ Lead in to the listening by asking when and why people change their careers. Elicit personal experiences of career changes. Ask: *Did you ever regret the changes you made?* Students listen to the four speakers and say which ones are happy with the changes they made.

Watch out! You might need to pre-teach the following.
antisocial hours = when you have to work at times of the day that make life difficult e.g. evenings, early mornings
army = the military force of a country
head of maths = lead teacher in the maths department at a school
secondary school = school attended by pupils aged 11–18
civil service = the administrative part of the government
high-powered = very important

> **Answers**
> Speakers 1 and 4 are unhappy, 2 and 3 are happy.

6 73▷ You may need to play the listening more than once for the students to be able to do this activity.

> **Answers**
> 1 strengths   4 challenge
> 2 weakness   5 ambition
> 3 career

7 Students match the words in **6** to the definitions.

> **Answers**
> 1 challenge(s)   4 career path
> 2 weakness(es)   5 ambition(s)
> 3 strengths

Tip Refer students to the *Tip* about *qualification, degree,* and *diploma*.

» If students need more practice, go to **Practice file 16** on page 132 of the **Student's Book**.

8 Students talk about their own career path using the ideas. Make it clear that they should talk about the past, present, and future.

Extension

Students make a poster of their career path, and post it on the wall. Students walk around and discuss the different paths. Did all the students represent their career path as a line?

Pre-work learners

This is a topic of particular importance to pre-work learners, and it would probably be beneficial to expand this activity. Clearly, one difference from in-work learners is that they have their entire career in front of them! Students should be encouraged to do some research on the Internet into their chosen career path (or go to the careers office in their place of study). They could research in detail how they will achieve their plans (e.g. by finding out about courses and diplomas in their chosen fields). They could be asked to write a report detailing what they are planning to do, and how they intend to achieve it.

Dictionary skills

British and American English: ask students to use their dictionaries to find the American English equivalents of these British English words and expressions.
Answers

at school	in school
rubbish	garbage / trash
autumn	fall
ground floor	first floor
mobile phone	cellphone
lorry	truck
holiday	vacation
underground	subway
a course (at college)	a program
bill	check
lift	elevator

ⓘ Refer students to the **Interactive Workbook Glossary** for further study.

Language at work

1 Write the title of the text on the board. Ask: what does *make a difference* mean in this context? (Suggested answer: *be useful to society*.) Students read the text and answer the question.

> **Answer**
> To give something back to the community

2 You may need to revise the grammatical terminology before students do the exercise. Students read the text again and find one example of each of the forms.

> **Answers**
> 2 money
> 3 have to
> 4 was sold
> 5 If you go back to studying, you'll find a job …
> 6 … would have more job satisfaction if they could give …
> 7 should (get in touch)

3 74▷ Students study the photos and speculate who the person may be and what he is doing. Explain the topic and ask students to read the questions. You could explain that Ulises de la Cruz is a real footballer who has played internationally for Ecuador and also in the English Premier League.

> **Answers**
> 1 He's a footballer.
> 2 From a poor village in the Chota valley in Ecuador
> 3 a new water system
>   a medical centre
>   books and a new roof for the school
>   the salaries of the doctor, nurse, and dentist
>   breakfast and lunch for all the schoolchildren

4 74▷ Students choose the correct answer and could then listen again to check their answers.

> **Answers**
> 1 sends   4 's building
> 2 grew up   5 'll open
> 3 's set up   6 's going to build

» If students need more practice, go to **Practice file 16** on page 133 of the **Student's Book**.

5 Students read the appropriate Files. They take turns to read out the sentences, and give their partner points for correct answers.

> **Answers**
> See Files 33 and 52 in the Student's Book.

Feedback focus
Ask the students to tell you why the incorrect ones are wrong.

Alternative
Mistakes auction: put the students in groups of three or four. Write out and copy ten sentences, five of which are correct and five have mistakes. (Make sure the mistakes come from the grammar in this book.) Students are 'given' £5,000 per group to spend in order to buy the correct sentences. Give them 10–15 minutes to discuss if the sentences are correct or not. Then 'auction' all 10 sentences one by one, with the highest bidder winning the sentence. The winner is the group with the largest number of correct sentences at the end. If two groups have the same number, the group with the most money left is the winner. NB make sure you spend ten minutes at the end getting the students to correct the wrong sentences.

6 Students may need to spend a few minutes inventing details about their 'friend's' CV. Make sure they present their friend in the best possible light. Explain that they will need to find out about the job as they go along and possibly make changes to their friend's profile to fit in with the job. The partner who has the job vacancy should spend a few minutes thinking of a specific job and some details about it.

Feedback focus
Focus on the grammar points from **2** and **4**. Write down any mistakes the students make with these points, and write them on the board at the end. Ask the students to correct their own mistakes.

Unit 16 Your career

Practically speaking

1 75▷ The students match the goodbyes to the responses. Then they listen and check.

Answers
1 b   2 d   3 a   4 c

2 75▷ The students listen again and decide if the conversations are formal or informal. They should write I or F next to the sentences. They could also note down expressions which helped them decide.

Answers
1 and 3 are informal, 2 and 4 are formal

3 Students practise using the phrases in the situations.

Suggested answers
1 Goodbye. Have a good trip.
2 Bye, see you on Monday.
3 It was nice meeting you.
4 Bye, I'm off.

Business communication

1 76▷ Ask the students to listen to the two presentations and answer the question.

Answers
Amy Chang

2 76▷ Play the presentations again and students answer the question.

Answers
2 Speaker 2   7 Speaker 2
3 Speaker 2   8 Speaker 1
4 Speaker 1   9 Speaker 2
5 Speaker 2   10 Speaker 1
6 Speaker 1

3 First ask students to underline the time phrase in sentence 1 (*last year*). Then ask them to do the same for all the sentences. Finally, ask them to write the time phrases in the correct column.

Answers

Talking about the past	Talking about recent experiences	Talking about the present	Talking about the future
Last year from 2002 to 2005 in my previous role	Recently up to now over the last year	in my current role at the moment	over the next year in the future

4 Give the students a few minutes to read their Files. They take turns to give presentations to each other.

Feedback focus
Focus on students' use of the time phrases from **3** and the correct tenses.

» If students need more practice, go to **Practice file 16** on page 132 of the **Student's Book**.

5 You may wish to give the students a fair amount of time to prepare their presentation. Encourage them to write notes for each category rather than full sentences. Ask them also to think about how to integrate the *Key expressions* with their personal information. Stronger students could be asked to make their presentation to the whole class.

Feedback focus
As for **4**.

Pronunciation
As with previous presentations, students will sound more natural in their delivery if they manage to 'chunk' their sentences. This means dividing up longer sentences into chunks of a few words (not more than seven, usually) and pausing slightly between them. Pauses should occur in natural places according to meaning, and each chunk should contain one (or possibly two) stresses, e.g.
I've been working // for my present company // for twenty years // on and off.

Extension
Students write out their presentation for homework using full sentences in paragraphs.

ⓘ Refer students to the **Interactive Workbook Email** and **Phrasebank** sections for further study and to the **Exercises and Tests** for revision.

Activity

The objective of this game is to practise the language and skills which the students have learned in this book. You may wish to ask students to revise this before they start the game.

Students read the rules of the game. Emphasize that the aim of the game is to review language and skills from the book.

You will probably find that students complete the tasks in the squares reasonably well, but without necessarily using the language from this book. In these cases, it is up to you whether you insist on them doing so, perhaps by looking it up in the second copy of the Student's Book as suggested.

As the students play, monitor carefully and help with queries about vocabulary.

Feedback focus

One way to give feedback is to keep a 'hot card' for each student, or each pair. As they play, write down errors on their hot card, and at the end, give them their hot card for discussion and correction. If you have a large class, you could ask students to monitor each other's mistakes, and fix a penalty of 'two squares back' for anybody who makes a mistake. If students disagree, for example about correct pronunciation, they ask you to decide.

» Unit 16 **Progress test** and **Speaking test**, pages 118–119.

1 | Progress test

Working with words

Choose the correct answer from the words in *italics*.

1 We offer many different services, but we *operate / specialize / produce* in cleaning and hygiene.

2 Adidas has several *competitors / subsidiaries / products*, including Reebok and Nike.

3 Generally speaking, our *employees / sales / makes* are very happy in their work.

4 The company is *operated / produced / based* in Slough, just outside London.

5 Last year, the company's *offers / sales / nationalities* increased by 10%.

Language at work

Complete the questions. Write one word in each space.

6 What _____ you do?

7 _____ are you here at the conference?

8 _____ your company operate in the UK?

9 How old _____ the company?

10 How _____ people work for the company?

Match the questions (6–10) to the answers (a–e). Write the number of the question next to the answer.

a About 30 years old.   11 ___

b I'm an engineer.   12 ___

c More than 600.   13 ___

d No, it doesn't.   14 ___

e To meet some of my customers. 15 ___

Correct the sentences. There is one mistake in each sentence.

16 Could you to speak more clearly?
_____

17 Would I have a glass of water, please?
_____

18 Can you giving me your address?
_____

19 Yes, of course not.
_____

20 Can you borrow me your mobile?
_____

Business communication

Put the conversation between Jack and Camille in order. Write a–j after each section (21–30). The first sentence is given.

Excuse me. Can I introduce myself? I'm Jack Reynolds.

21 I'm an IT engineer. I work with computers and IT systems. What do *you* do? ___

22 How do you do? Where are you from, Camille? ___

23 To repair the computers! ___

24 Camille Vargas. I'm sorry. It's nice to meet you, but I must go now. ___

25 I'm French. I live in Marseilles. How about you? ___

26 Oh right. Can I introduce to you to my colleague Peter Samms? His computer's not working very well, and maybe … Peter, this is … sorry what's your name again? ___

27 I'm from Detroit in the United States. What do you do? ___

28 I'm a TV reporter. I work for CNN in their Detroit office. Why are you here at the trade fair? ___

29 How do you do? I'm Camille Vargas. ___

30 OK, Camille, see you later. ___

Result _____ / 30 marks

Speaking test

Role cards

Copy this page and cut out the role cards for the students. Then use the *Speaking test results* forms to evaluate each student's performance. You can then cut out the results and give them to the students.

Cut along this line

Student A

Your company: *Brushwood Systems* – makes telephone systems – 3,500 employees – based in Sydney, Australia – operates in sixteen countries – main competitors are Siemens.

You meet Student B at a conference. You do not know each other.

- Introduce yourself.
- Find out the other person's name, job, and company.
- Tell them what your company does and some information about it.
- Ask why they are at the conference.
- Ask if you can take their name and telephone number.

Student B

Your company: *Sweet and Savoury* – provides food and drink services – specializes in providing food to film companies – 250 employees – based in Leeds, UK – operates in the UK and Ireland – main competitors are DirectFood.

You meet Student A at a conference. You do not know each other.

- Introduce yourself.
- Find out the other person's name, job, and company.
- Tell them what your company does and some information about it.
- Ask why they are at the conference.
- Ask if they can give you a business card.

Cut along this line

Speaking test results

Use these forms to evaluate the students.

Cut along this line

Student A

Can the student …	Didn't do this (0 points)	Yes, but with some mistakes (1 point)	Yes, did this very well (2 points)
introduce themselves and greet the other person?			
ask about the other person's job or company?			
talk about their own job or company?			
ask and answer why they are at the conference?			
make a polite request?			

Result _____ / 10 marks

Student B

Can the student …	Didn't do this (0 points)	Yes, but with some mistakes (1 point)	Yes, did this very well (2 points)
introduce themselves and greet the other person?			
ask about the other person's job or company?			
talk about their own job or company?			
ask and answer why they are at the conference?			
make a polite request?			

Result _____ / 10 marks

Cut along this line

Photocopiable © Oxford University Press

2 | Progress test

Working with words

Write sentences using the words.

1 I / not / involved / talk / customers.
   _____

2 Sarah / deal / software issues.
   _____

3 My job / consist / telephone / suppliers.
   _____

4 / you ever / take part / meetings and discussions / subcontractors?
   _____

5 Peter's work / involve / organize / travel / colleagues.
   _____

Write the words after the definitions.

6 an organization that finds staff for another company
   _____ _____

7 a company or person that buys your product _____

8 a person who deals with the image of a company
   _____ _____ _____

9 companies that do work for you that you can't do yourself
   _____

10 a person who you work with _____

11 a company that sells its products to you _____

12 an expert from outside the company who gives advice and help _____

Language at work

Choose the correct answer from the words in *italics*.

13 This week John *works* / *is working* on a big contract with Nike.

14 How often *does your company work* / *is your company working* with outside consultants?

15 Sorry I can't speak to you now, I *expect* / *'m expecting* a call from our Paris office.

16 *Are you working* / *Do you work* very hard at the moment?

17 The Sales Director *uses* / *is using* this room every Tuesday.

18 I can't give you a decision at this time. The Sales Director *thinks* / *is thinking* about your proposal.

19 Hello, this is a message for Paul Timms. Paul, I *just leave* / *'m just leaving* now. I'll be with you in about ten minutes.

20 The main problem with my job is that it *doesn't involve* / *isn't involving* any contact with the customers.

Business communication

Complete the telephone conversation with words from the list.

| about | afraid | back | calling | course |
| leave | phoning | speak | this | welcome |

A Could I 21_____ to Ms Rosie Walton, please?

B Who's 22_____?

A 23_____ is Tom Jacks from ATC.

B Could you tell me what it's 24_____?

A I'm 25_____ to invite Rosie to our anniversary lunch next month.

B Well, I'm 26_____ Ms Walton is out of the office at the moment.

A Oh. In that case, could I 27_____ a message?

B Yes, of 28_____.

A Can you ask Rosie to call me 29_____?

B Yes, does she have your number?

A Yes, she does.

B OK, I'll give her your message.

A Thanks very much.

B You're 30_____.

Result _____ / 30 marks

Speaking test

Role cards

Copy this page and cut out the role cards for the students. Then use the *Speaking test results* forms to evaluate each student's performance. You can then cut out the results and give them to the students.

Student A

1 You work for a marketing agency. You are doing research on consumer buying. You want to speak to the Sales Manager of a clothing retailer to find out about their customers and market segments. Call Student B:
- Introduce yourself.
- Ask to speak to the Sales Manager.
- Explain why you are calling.
- Ask to leave a message.
- Give your phone number.
- Thank them and say goodbye.

2 You work in the Finance Department. Student B telephones you.
- Answer the call.
- Say that the Accounts assistant is very busy at the moment dealing with other colleagues.
- Offer to take a message.

Student B

1 You work for a clothing retailer. Student A telephones you.
- Answer the call.
- Say that the Sales Manager is in a meeting.
- Offer to take a message.

2 You need to fill in your expenses form, but it is very complicated. Call the Finance department for help:
- Introduce yourself.
- Say why you are calling.
- Ask to speak to the Accounts assistant.
- Ask to leave a message.
- Give your phone number.
- Say goodbye.

Speaking test results

Use these forms to evaluate the students.

Student A

Can the student …	Didn't do this (0 points)	Yes, but with some mistakes (1 point)	Yes, did this very well (2 points)
introduce him/herself on the phone?			
explain why he/she is calling?			
leave a message?			
take a message?			
end a phone call?			

Result _____ / 10 marks

Student B

Can the student …	Didn't do this (0 points)	Yes, but with some mistakes (1 point)	Yes, did this very well (2 points)
introduce him/herself on the phone?			
explain why he/she is calling?			
leave a message?			
take a message?			
end a phone call?			

Result _____ / 10 marks

Photocopiable © Oxford University Press

3 | Progress test

Working with words

Which department do these people work in?

1 Arthur installs programs on the company PCs. _____
2 Lara interviews applicants for jobs. _____
3 Silvana buys office equipment for the whole group. _____
4 Akira runs courses in Japanese. _____
5 Pablo deals with transporting goods to the customer. _____
6 Marcel checks the products for faults. _____
7 If you have a broken photocopier, call Mike. _____
8 Tatiana is in charge of a team looking for new ideas. _____
9 Dieter looks after the money. _____
10 Tina finds out what the customers really want. _____

Language at work

Write the questions for the answers. Use the correct form of the word in brackets.

11 I work in HR. (department)
   _____?
12 About 15,000. (employ)
   _____?
13 I'm planning a trip to Hong Kong. (at the moment)
   _____?
14 Tea, please. (prefer)
   _____?
15 About six times a year. (visit Japan)
   _____?
16 He's Swedish. (come)
   _____?
17 I'm here until next Thursday. (stay)
   _____?
18 In 2005. (move here)
   _____?
19 Not very much. (know about the Australian market)
   _____?
20 Parts for car engines. (produce)
   _____?

Business communication

Complete this presentation with phrases a–j.

a everybody see
b increase
c that clear
d important thing here
e a breakdown of
f shows
g let's look
h notice that
i a look at
j you can see

Have ²¹___ this graph. Is ²²___ ? This graph ²³___ the money we have spent on salaries in the last ten years. As ²⁴___, there has been a big ²⁵___ overall, from €250,000 to €400,000, but the ²⁶___ is that per head salaries have only risen 3%.

²⁷___ at the next slide. Can ²⁸___ that? This pie chart gives ²⁹___ spending on salaries by region. ³⁰___ Europe is 20% higher than anywhere else.

Result _____ / 30 marks

Speaking test

Role card

This *Speaking test* has only one role card because each student has to give a presentation. Copy this page and cut out the role card for the student. Then use the *Speaking test results* forms to evaluate the student's performance. You can then cut out the results and give them to the student.

Cut along this line

You work for a stationery company. You manufacture office equipment and supply it to companies in Western Europe and Asia. You are presenting the findings of an internal report about your company, its products, and its markets in order to find a strategy for the future. Use this table and present the information.

Strengths	Weaknesses
• Clients trust the product and service • Good sales teams • Good product range	• High price compared to some competitors • Supply chain is unreliable
Opportunities	**Threats**
• Emerging markets in Eastern Europe • Potential new partnerships with producers in the East	• Economic situation is unstable • Cost of raw materials is increasing

- Introduce the presentation
- Explain what the table represents
- Check that the table is visible
- Describe each section individually
- Focus on one or two important points

Cut along this line

Speaking test results

Use this form to evaluate the student.

Cut along this line

Can the student …	Didn't do this (0 points)	Yes, but with some mistakes (1 point)	Yes, did this very well (2 points)
introduce the presentation?			
explain the visual information?			
check it is visible?			
describe the visual information in detail?			
focus on important points?			

Result _____ / 10 marks

Cut along this line

Photocopiable © Oxford University Press

4 | Progress test

Working with words

Complete the text with words from the list.

| cheap | compact | designed | did | friendly |
| idea | launched | stylish | trials | well |

An electronics company wanted to develop a new product for the British market. They had an ¹_____ for a calculator with big keys, so that older people could use it easily, but which was ²_____ so that it could fit into a pocket or bag. They ³_____ some market research and found that people would buy it if it was ⁴_____-designed and quite ⁵_____ – no more than £10. They ⁶_____ the product and asked a research company called TBT to do some product ⁷_____. These found that the new calculator was very popular with younger people too, as they thought the bright colours and big keys were very ⁸_____. The company ⁹_____ the product two years ago, and it has been a great success: older people find it user-¹⁰_____, while teenagers love its 'look'.

Language at work

Write a positive sentence (+), a negative sentence (-), or a question (?) from the prompts. Use the past simple.

11 Felipe / go / to Paris yesterday (-)
    _____

12 you / see / the new consultants / last week (?)
    _____

13 I / receive / your letter (-)
    _____

14 The sales team / meet / the new director this morning (+)
    _____

15 the product / have / any success at the conference (?)
    _____

Correct the mistakes in the sentences.

16 We didn't found the presentation very interesting.
    _____

17 The company buyed a lot of new furniture.
    _____

18 Francesca not enjoyed the meal with the sales manager.
    _____

19 They arrive at the airport at 6 p.m. yesterday.
    _____

20 The report didn't be very informative.
    _____

Business communication

A supermarket wants to change its supplier of fresh fruit and vegetables. The purchasing department has prepared a report. Order the report. Write a–j after the sentences.

21 First, we did some research to find the cheapest suppliers in the market. ___

22 Why did we need to change supplier? ___

23 We found that it was excellent. ___

24 The purpose of our research was to find a new supplier of fresh fruit and vegetables to all our stores. ___

25 We spoke to about twenty different companies, and found that Greenpark were 5–10% cheaper than anyone else. ___

26 We asked them to send us some information, and invited them to a meeting. ___

27 Finally, we contacted Greenpark, who seemed friendly and well-organized. ___

28 Because our previous one was expensive, and sometimes didn't deliver the goods on time. ___

29 Then we asked some of our sister companies how good the reliability of Greenpark was. ___

30 We wanted to find a supplier that was cheap and reliable. ___

Result _____ / 30 marks

Speaking test

Role cards

Copy this page and cut out the role cards for the students. Then use the *Speaking test results* forms to evaluate each student's performance. You can then cut out the results and give them to the students.

Cut along this line

Student A

1 Give a report to Student B about a new product using this information. Student B will then ask you some questions about the report. Invent sensible answers to B's questions.

- new product: new drink, mixture of yoghurt and fruit
- reason for new product: gap in the market
- timing of market research and product trials: last year

2 Student B will give you a similar report. You should respond to the information with appropriate phrases showing interest. After he / she finishes, ask questions to find out this information:

- when they did the market research and product trials
- what the final result of the research was.

Student B

1 Student A will give you a report about a new product. You should respond to the information with appropriate phrases showing interest. After he / she finishes, ask questions to find out this information:

- when they launched the new product
- what the final result was.

2 Give a similar report to Student A using this information. Student A will then ask you some questions about the report. Invent sensible answers to A's questions.

- new product: wireless headset for Internet phones
- reason for new product: people want a cheap and functional headset
- timing of launch: last month

Cut along this line

Speaking test results

Use these forms to evaluate the students.

Cut along this line

Student A

Can the student …	Didn't do this (0 points)	Yes, but with some mistakes (1 point)	Yes, did this very well (2 points)
give a simple but coherent report?			
use some or all of the report phrases from the unit?			
talk about the development of a product?			
ask and answer questions in the past simple?			
show interest in the other person's report?			

Result _____ / 10 marks

Student B

Can the student …	Didn't do this (0 points)	Yes, but with some mistakes (1 point)	Yes, did this very well (2 points)
give a simple but coherent report?			
use some or all of the report phrases from the unit?			
talk about the development of a product?			
ask and answer questions in the past simple?			
show interest in the other person's report?			

Result _____ / 10 marks

Cut along this line

Photocopiable © Oxford University Press

5 | Progress test

Working with words

Complete the sentences. Write one word in each space.

1 Unfortunately we cannot pay an annual b_____ this year.
2 I need to u_____ my CV before I apply for the job.
3 We have fifteen candidates on the s_____ for interviews.
4 My company gives six months of maternity l_____ if you have a baby.
5 We get s_____ childcare, which is very useful.
6 You need to fill in an application f_____.
7 Most big companies have a pension s_____ for their employees.
8 There is a vacancy for the p_____ of Director of Marketing.
9 Flexible h_____ are good for me, because I have to take the children to school before I start work.
10 He saw a job a_____ in the newspaper.

Language at work

Order the words to make sentences or questions in the present perfect or past simple. (2 points each)

11 applied / for / have / job / the / yet / you / ?
_____

12 already / company / CV / have / I / my / sent / the / to
_____

13 any / did / get / holiday / last / not / paid / they / year
_____

14 been / France / has / month / she / this / to / ?
_____

15 did / job / last / leave / when / you / your / ?
_____

Business communication

Complete the emails with phrases from the list. There are TWO phrases that you will not need.

deal with it	I haven't	running out	has he
where are we	I talked	leave it to	what about
did he	have you done	short of time	I didn't

Hi Yumiko
16 _____ with the new photocopier? The training course is starting next week, so time's
17 _____. 18 _____ anything about it?
Don

Don
I'm sorry, I've been 19 _____ this week.
Can you 20 _____?
Yumiko

Dear Yumiko
Yes, 21 _____ me. And 22 _____ the problem with the cleaners? 23 _____ to Ed Norris at CleanYouUp yesterday. 24 _____ called back?
Don

Don,
No, 25 _____ heard from him yet.
Y.

Result _____ / 30 marks

Speaking test

Role cards

Copy this page and cut out the role cards for the students. Then use the *Speaking test results* forms to evaluate each student's performance. You can then cut out the results and give them to the students.

Cut along this line

Student A

You are working on a proposal for new company benefits. Have a meeting to discuss your progress on the following tasks.

Your tasks:

Research what other companies in the industry do – *did last week*
Send questionnaire to staff members – *sent two days ago*
Write a report on your findings, deadline next week – *not done (need results of questionnaires)*

Student B's tasks:

Interview heads of department
Talk to HR about all current benefits
Write report, deadline next week

- Ask Student B about his / her progress
- Describe your own progress
- Say if something is urgent
- Decide who will do what now
- Summarize your discussion

Student B

You are working on a proposal for new company benefits. Have a meeting to discuss your progress on the following tasks.

Your tasks:

Interview heads of department – *not finished yet*
Talk to HR about all current benefits – *did yesterday*
Write report, deadline next week – *not done (need information from interviews)*

Student A's tasks:

Research what other companies in the industry do
Send questionnaire to staff members
Write a report on the findings, deadline next week

- Ask Student A about his / her progress
- Describe your own progress
- Say if something is urgent
- Decide who will do what now
- Summarize your discussion

Cut along this line

Speaking test results

Use these forms to evaluate the students.

Cut along this line

Student A

Can the student …	Didn't do this (0 points)	Yes, but with some mistakes (1 point)	Yes, did this very well (2 points)
ask about progress?			
describe his / her progress?			
explain the urgency of a task?			
decide who will do what?			
summarize what has been agreed?			

Result _____ / 10 marks

Student B

Can the student …	Didn't do this (0 points)	Yes, but with some mistakes (1 point)	Yes, did this very well (2 points)
ask about progress?			
describe his / her progress?			
explain the urgency of a task?			
decide who will do what?			
summarize what has been agreed?			

Result _____ / 10 marks

Cut along this line

Photocopiable © Oxford University Press

6 | Progress test

Working with words

Read the text and choose the correct answer from the words in *italics*.

Our company does everything to ¹*meet / keep* the needs of our customers. As the leading online electronics retailer, it is important we always ²*agree / keep* to our delivery dates, and get the goods to our customers ³*on time / in time*. When we receive complaints about this, we make sure we ⁴*provide / deal* with them immediately. Sometimes we have to give customers their money ⁵*away / back*.

Of course, we try to ⁶*design / encourage* customer loyalty in various ways – for example, returning clients receive a 10% discount on the second order. In a survey that we ⁷*made / conducted* last year, we found that 98% of our customers are ⁸*satisfied / reliable*. But we want to do better, and we are now looking at ways of offering a ⁹*personalized / loyal* service to our long-term clients. Above all, it's vital to ¹⁰*provide / design* the service that people want.

Language at work

Correct the mistakes.

11 This is the goodest restaurant in town.
   _____

12 The job was not as easier as we expected.
   _____

13 Marcia's most hard-working employee in this company.
   _____

14 Our sales figures are the most low they've been for twenty years.
   _____

15 Our rival BJT has the bigest market share.
   _____

16 Market conditions are more difficulter than last year.
   _____

17 The less profitable of our three divisions is Europe.
   _____

18 We need to think of ways of making our staff happyer.
   _____

19 Can you be carefuller in future?
   _____

20 The new building is best than the old one in many ways.
   _____

Business communication

Aseel and Emre are discussing the installation of a new water cooling machine. Complete the conversation following the instructions in the brackets. (2 points each)

Aseel I see they're thinking of installing a new water cooler in Reception. *(ask Emre's opinion)*
21 _____?

Emre I don't like the idea. *(give an opinion)*
22 _____ that water coolers are a waste of money.

Aseel *(disagree strongly)*
23 _____. It's good that customers can get a drink while they're waiting.

Emre *(agree)* 24 _____. But not in Reception! It will get really dirty. And what about all the empty plastic cups? It's not very green.

Aseel *(agree strongly)*
25 _____. Maybe we could bring our own cups?

Result _____ / 30 marks

Speaking test

Role cards

Copy this page and cut out the role cards for the students. Then use the *Speaking test results* forms to evaluate each student's performance. You can then cut out the results and give them to the students.

Cut along this line

Student A

Your company is losing customers. Talk to Student B to discuss ways in which you can get them back.

- Compare your company's performance with your competitors.
- Make suggestions from the list of ideas below, and ask for the other person's opinion.
- Give your opinion of the other person's ideas, including agreeing and disagreeing.
- Decide together which two of the ideas are the best.

Possible ideas:

- 20% discount to loyal customers
- free present with every order over £100
- automatic refund for every customer who complains
- more staff in the call centre to answer calls

Student B

Your company is losing customers. Talk to Student A to discuss ways in which you can get them back.

- Compare your company's performance with your competitors.
- Make suggestions from the list of ideas below, and ask for the other person's opinion.
- Give your opinion of the other person's ideas, including agreeing and disagreeing.
- Decide together which two of the ideas are the best.

Possible ideas:

- special credit card for loyal customers
- conduct surveys every month to find out what customers want
- change the supplier who delivers your goods
- promise 50% discount on next order if we are late with delivery

Cut along this line

Speaking test results

Use these forms to evaluate the students.

Cut along this line

Student A

Can the student …	Didn't do this (0 points)	Yes, but with some mistakes (1 point)	Yes, did this very well (2 points)
use the vocabulary of customer service?			
compare companies?			
ask for an opinion?			
give an opinion?			
agree and disagree politely?			

Result _____ / 10 marks

Student B

Can the student …	Didn't do this (0 points)	Yes, but with some mistakes (1 point)	Yes, did this very well (2 points)
use the vocabulary of customer service?			
compare companies?			
ask for an opinion?			
give an opinion?			
agree and disagree politely?			

Result _____ / 10 marks

Cut along this line

Photocopiable © Oxford University Press

Unit 6 Tests

7 | Progress test

Working with words

Complete the text with one word in each space.

My ¹t_____ to the USA last week did not go well. First of all, when I arrived at the airport, I was told that my ²f_____ was ³d_____ for two hours. I didn't want to wait in the ⁴t_____ , so I ⁵c_____ in to a Yotel. Unfortunately, when I came to pay my ⁶b_____ I found I had left my credit card at home.

Eventually, back at the airport, we passed through the ⁷g_____ and waited in the ⁸d_____ lounge. I ⁹b_____ the plane about three hours late. But my troubles were not over. When we got to Boston, I found that my ¹⁰l_____ had gone to Seattle!

Complete the sentences.

11 Before you check out of the hotel, please remember to bring your k_____ c_____ to Reception.

12 You should leave your valuables in the s_____ in your room.

13 Would you like a o_____ ticket or a return?

14 I took the s_____ bus from the hotel to the airport.

Language at work

Write a question with the word in brackets in the correct form for each answer.

15 _____ near here? (hotel)

Yes, there's one just down this street.

16 _____ have you got? (luggage)

Just a suitcase and a handbag.

17 _____ have you been to Beijing? (time)

More than twenty. I first went there when I was working for HSBC.

18 _____ at this time of night? (taxi)

Yes, there are lots.

19 _____ do you do in a year? (travel)

Quite a lot. I go abroad once or twice a month.

20 _____ to do any shopping? (time)

Yes, we've got a couple of hours free tomorrow.

Business communication

Complete the sentences. Write one word in each space.

21 Have you _____ to Oslo before?

22 _____ was your flight?

23 What _____ of food do you like?

24 Where _____ you go on holiday last year?

25 How often do you _____ sailing?

26 Is this your first _____ to Sydney?

27 _____ you have a good journey?

28 Does your wife travel a lot _____ business?

29 _____ you interested in football?

30 What did you _____ of the food last night?

Result _____ / 30 marks

Speaking test

Role cards

Copy this page and cut out the role cards for the students. Then use the *Speaking test results* forms to evaluate each student's performance. You can then cut out the results and give them to the students.

Cut along this line

Student A

1 You work for Devla plc. You meet Student B at the airport. You do not know each other.
   - Introduce yourself and say who you work for.
   - Ask B about his / her flight.
   - Ask if he / she has been to your city before.
   - Answer his / her questions.

2 You work for Tetra plc. You are visiting Student B who meets you at the airport. You do not know each other.
   - Introduce yourself and say who you work for.
   - Respond to B's questions.
   - Ask B about restaurants in the city.
   - Ask B two questions about his / her interests / habits.

Student B

1 You work for Starworld plc. You are visiting Student A who meets you at the airport. You do not know each other.
   - Introduce yourself and say who you work for.
   - Respond to A's questions.
   - Ask about A's city.
   - Ask A two questions about his / her interests / habits.

2 You work for Silverfish plc. You meet Student A at the airport. You do not know each other.
   - Introduce yourself and say who you work for.
   - Ask A about his / her flight.
   - Ask if he / she has been to your city before.
   - Answer his / her questions.

Cut along this line

Speaking test results

Use these forms to evaluate the students.

Cut along this line

Student A

Can the student …	Didn't do this (0 points)	Yes, but with some mistakes (1 point)	Yes, did this very well (2 points)
introduce him / herself and say which company he / she is from?			
ask about the other person's journey?			
ask about their city?			
ask appropriate small talk questions?			
answer questions to develop a conversation?			

Result _____ / 10 marks

Student B

Can the student …	Didn't do this (0 points)	Yes, but with some mistakes (1 point)	Yes, did this very well (2 points)
introduce him / herself and say which company he / she is from?			
ask about the other person's journey?			
ask about their city?			
ask appropriate small talk questions?			
answer questions to develop a conversation?			

Result _____ / 10 marks

Cut along this line

Unit 7 Tests

Photocopiable © Oxford University Press

101

8 | Progress test

Working with words

Complete the texts with words from the list.

complaint	delivered	gave	invoice
make	place	process	purchased
quote	stock	track	

Is it true that the Internet has changed the way we shop? OK, we can look at a website, see something we like, and check if the item is in ¹_____. But is this so different from simply telephoning? And then, when we ²_____ the order, we don't need to talk to anybody – the order goes through and we wait for the product to arrive at our door. But 100 years ago, you sent a message to a shop, and they ³_____ the goods the same afternoon. So what's new? You still have to pay the ⁴_____!

The best thing about online shopping is the fact that you can ⁵_____ your shipment. When I ⁶_____ some goods last month for my company, I really needed to know when they would arrive. Of course, the website ⁷_____ me a date for delivery, but the company don't ⁸_____ their orders very quickly, so I wanted to check every day.

Sometimes, you ⁹_____ an enquiry about a product, the suppliers ¹⁰_____ you a price for it, and everything seems fine. But then the goods don't arrive, and you need to make a ¹¹_____. This can be very frustrating.

Language at work

Complete the conversation with the correct form (*will*, *going to*, or present continuous) of the verb in brackets.

Anna Hi, Jean. ¹²_____ (you / do) anything this evening?

Jean Yes, I think I ¹³_____ (stay) at home and watch TV. Why?

Anna Well, Milos and I ¹⁴_____ (go) out for a drink with our new boss, and we wanted to invite you.

Jean Your new boss?

Anna Yes, her name's Jessica, and she ¹⁵_____ (start) next week. We're going to that new bar on 22nd Street.

Jean In that case, I ¹⁶_____ (come) with you! I've always wanted to go there. What time ¹⁷_____ (you / meet)?

Anna About six.

Jean I ¹⁸_____ (bring) Tony. He'd like to meet Jessica.

Anna I'm not sure about that. Jessica's his ex-wife!

Jean Oh no. OK, I ¹⁹_____ (not / say) anything about it.

Business communication

Complete the exchanges. Write one word in each space.

1 **A** We don't have any envelopes. ²⁰_____ we get some more?

   B I'm not sure ²¹_____ that. Jack just ordered some.

2 **A** How ²²_____ going out for a meal?

   B That's a ²³_____ idea! ²⁴_____ go to Nando's.

   A Yes, I think we ²⁵_____ book a table.

3 **A** The photocopier's broken again!

   B Why ²⁶_____ we try a new supplier this time?

   A Fine. We ²⁷_____ phone that new shop in Market Street.

   B I don't ²⁸_____ that will work. It closed down last week!

4 **A** The new man in Reception seems a bit unhappy. I ²⁹_____ you have a word with him.

   B OK. Maybe we ³⁰_____ invite him out for a drink on Friday.

Result _____ / 30 marks

Speaking test

Role cards

Copy this page and cut out the role cards for the students. Then use the *Speaking test results* forms to evaluate each student's performance. You can then cut out the results and give them to the students.

Cut along this line

Student A

Your department manager will celebrate ten years with the company next month, and you are organizing a party for her. Talk to Student B about the party. You want a big party with lots of people.

- Suggest places you could hold the party.
- Decide who you are going to invite.
- Decide who will organize the party.
- Arrange a meeting next week to plan the party in more detail.

These are some possibilities:

Where?
A night club in town (holds 160 people)
Company meeting room (holds 60 people)
Who to invite?
All current staff members (56 people)
Everyone who worked in her department in the last 10 years (150 people)

Student B

Your department manager will celebrate ten years with the company next month, and you are organizing a party for her. Talk to Student A about the party. You think she would prefer a small party.

- Suggest places you could hold the party.
- Decide who you are going to invite.
- Decide who will organize the party.
- Arrange a meeting next week to plan the party in more detail.

These are some possibilities:

Where?
Company meeting room (holds 60 people)
A restaurant (holds 30 people)
Who to invite?
All current staff members (56 people)
Her current department (17 people)

Cut along this line

Speaking test results

Use these forms to evaluate the students.

Cut along this line

Student A

Can the student …	Didn't do this (0 points)	Yes, but with some mistakes (1 point)	Yes, did this very well (2 points)
make a suggestion?			
accept a suggestion?			
reject a suggestion?			
say what he / she is going to do?			
arrange to meet?			

Result _____ / 10 marks

Student B

Can the student …	Didn't do this (0 points)	Yes, but with some mistakes (1 point)	Yes, did this very well (2 points)
make a suggestion?			
accept a suggestion?			
reject a suggestion?			
say what he / she is going to do?			
arrange to meet?			

Result _____ / 10 marks

Cut along this line

Photocopiable © Oxford University Press

Unit 8 Tests

9 | Progress test

Working with words

Choose the correct answer from the words in *italics*.

1 Carrefour *improved / entered / boosted* the Chinese market in 1995.
2 The best way to *attract / offer / launch* customers is to cut prices!
3 We need an advertising *mail / campaign / outdoor* to promote our new range.
4 The best way of advertising is by word of *recommendation / truth / mouth*.
5 The company *advertised / boosted / promoted* its sales by putting fresh fruit in its stores.
6 It increased its market *share / position / sales* by 10% last year.
7 We have decided to *set / put / launch* five new products next year.
8 John works in *ads / advertisement / advertising*.
9 *Direct / Outdoor / Loyalty* mailing is a very simple way of advertising.
10 They have to *offer / expand / share* their range of services if they want to succeed.

Language at work

It is Min's first day at work. Complete the conversation with a colleague with the correct form of *have to, need to, can*, or *allowed to*.

Min I see you're wearing a tie. Do I ⁱ¹_____ wear one?
Dag No, you ¹²_____ wear whatever you like. But you ¹³_____ look smart if you're meeting customers.
Min I guess we ¹⁴_____ (not) smoke in here?
Dag Absolutely not. There's a part of the garden where you ¹⁵_____ smoke. And you ¹⁶_____ (not) to drink tea or coffee in any of the work areas – that's not possible at all.
Min So what time ¹⁷_____ to start in the morning?
Dag Most people start at 8.30, but you ¹⁸_____ arrive at work any time until 10 a.m. But you ¹⁹_____ to stay after 6.30 p.m., because they close the building then.
Min And what do I call my line manager?
Dag Don't worry – you ²⁰_____ call him Mr Jones. We all call him Frank.

Business communication

Complete the expressions with the correct form of a verb from the list.

| be   catch   come back   could   cover |
| discuss   get off   move on   say   sum up |

21 We can _____ to that later.
22 Can we _____ to point number 2 on the agenda?
23 I'd like to _____ what we've agreed.
24 I'm so sorry. What was that you _____?
25 We're here today to _____ the new advertising campaign.
26 I'm sorry, but I think we're _____ the subject.
27 It's six o'clock, and we've _____ everything.
28 I didn't really understand that. _____ you be more specific?
29 I _____ not with you there.
30 Say that again – I didn't _____ that.

Result _____ / 30 marks

Speaking test

Role cards

Copy this page and cut out the role cards for the students. Then use the *Speaking test results* forms to evaluate each student's performance. You can then cut out the results and give them to the students.

Cut along this line

Student A

You and Student B work for a mobile phone company which is about to launch a new phone aimed at young people from 11–14. Discuss with him / her the best way to advertise and promote the new phone. Here are some ideas:

- TV advertising between 4 and 8 p.m., especially on music and video shows
- online ads on instant messaging services
- outdoor advertising near schools
- free stickers given out at school gates.

Choose TWO of these ideas to promote at the meeting.

- Talk about what the company has to do with the campaign.
- Get your point across – interrupt him / her if necessary, but don't let him / her interrupt you too much.
- Don't let him / her get off the subject – you don't want the meeting to last too long.
- Ask him / her to be more specific or repeat something.

Student B

You and Student A work for a mobile phone company which is about to launch a new phone aimed at young people from 11–14. Discuss with him / her the best way to advertise and promote the new phone. Here are some ideas:

- TV advertising between 4 and 8 p.m., especially on music and video shows
- online ads on instant messaging services
- outdoor advertising near schools
- free stickers given out at school gates.

Choose TWO of these ideas to promote at the meeting.

- Talk about what the company has to do with the campaign.
- Get your point across – interrupt him / her if necessary, but don't let him / her interrupt you too much.
- Don't let him / her get off the subject – you don't want the meeting to last too long.
- Ask him / her to be more specific or repeat something.

Cut along this line

Speaking test results

Use these forms to evaluate the students.

Cut along this line

Student A

Can the student …	Didn't do this (0 points)	Yes, but with some mistakes (1 point)	Yes, did this very well (2 points)
discuss advertising strategies?			
say what it is necessary to do?			
use the language of meetings?			
interrupt somebody?			
ask somebody to repeat or be more specific?			

Result _____ / 10 marks

Student B

Can the student …	Didn't do this (0 points)	Yes, but with some mistakes (1 point)	Yes, did this very well (2 points)
discuss advertising strategies?			
say what it is necessary to do?			
use the language of meetings?			
interrupt somebody?			
ask somebody to repeat or be more specific?			

Result _____ / 10 marks

Cut along this line

Photocopiable © Oxford University Press

10 | Progress test

Working with words

Complete the sentences with a word from the list.

> convenient   effective   friendly   initiative
> original   popular   recycled   unusual
> useful   value

1 This is the most _____ computer in our range – over 1 million were sold last year.

2 We need to use environmentally-_____ products in the new factory.

3 The company has started an _____ to reduce waste by 20% over ten years.

4 This shop is very _____ – only five minutes' walk from here.

5 These shoes were expensive, but they've been good _____ for money as they've lasted so long.

6 The management is 100% women, which is very _____, even nowadays.

7 Most companies have a box near the photocopier for waste paper to be _____.

8 The sales campaign was not very _____ – we've only managed to sell 600.

9 His ideas for going green are completely _____ – I've never seen any of them before.

10 Thank you very much for your very _____ suggestions.

Language at work

Read the description of the recycling of glass, and put the verbs in brackets in the correct tense in the active or the passive.

In the past, not many bottles 11_____ (recycle), but nowadays, people 12_____ (want) to be green, and 13_____ (take) their empty bottles to the bottle bank. From there, the bottles 14_____ (collect) and 15_____ (transport) by lorry to the recycling centre. A large furnace 16_____ (melt) the bottles at very high temperatures. The melted glass 17_____ (make) into new bottles, which 18_____ (buy) by drinks companies. The companies 19_____ (fill) the bottles with new drinks and the bottles 20_____ (sell) to supermarkets.

Business communication

Correct the sentences from the presentation.

21 I'll talk about that after.
_____

22 That brings to my next point.
_____

23 First all, I'd like to say a few words about recycling.
_____

24 Thanks very much for listen today.
_____

25 My next points is about company image.
_____

26 As I say before, the problem is complicated.
_____

27 I'm here today tell you about the benefits of carbon offsetting.
_____

28 Let's move in to my next point.
_____

29 Good afternoon somebody.
_____

30 We're going to looking at the subject of carbon emissions.
_____

Result _____ / 30 marks

106

Photocopiable © Oxford University Press

Speaking test

Role card

This *Speaking test* has only one role card because each student has to give an individual presentation. Copy this page and cut out the role card for the student. Then use the *Speaking test results* form to evaluate the student's performance. You can then cut out the results and give them to the student.

Cut along this line

You are in charge of green policy at your place of work or study.

1 Prepare a list of three new initiatives that you think your place of work or study should adopt.
2 Now prepare and give a short (five-minute) presentation. Follow these stages:
   - Give a brief overview of your place of work (or study).
   - Explain your ideas for new green initiatives, and for each one, say why you think they are a good idea, and possible disadvantages.

Don't forget to use the language of presentations appropriately, including
   - starting the presentation
   - moving on to another subject
   - referring backwards and forwards
   - finishing the presentation.

You do not need to use visual aids.

Cut along this line

Speaking test results

Use this form to evaluate the student.

Cut along this line

Can the student …	Didn't do this (0 points)	Yes, but with some mistakes (1 point)	Yes, did this very well (2 points)
start the presentation?			
use the vocabulary of green issues appropriately?			
move from one topic to another?			
refer backwards and forwards?			
close the presentation?			

Result _____ / 10 marks

Cut along this line

Photocopiable © Oxford University Press

11 | Progress test

Working with words

Choose the correct answer from the words in *italics*.

1. The company is planning a corporate *event / venue* next July.
2. The *venue / trip* for this will be the Open Golf Championship.
3. We are going to *offer / entertain* our clients over three days.
4. On the first evening, *hosts / guests* will attend a luxury buffet supper.
5. For the second day, we have *booked / accepted* golf lessons with a local professional golfer.
6. On the third day, a trip to a local whisky producer has been *arranged / held*.
7. We are going to send out *offers / invitations* to selected clients next week.
8. We think that about 50–70 people will *accept / book*.
9. You may ask: what is the *event / purpose* of the project?
10. It is to *hold / reinforce* our relationships with our most important clients.

Language at work

Write the correct form of the verbs.

a. If the weather ¹¹_____ (be) good tomorrow, they ¹²_____ (play) the match.

b. What ¹³_____ (you / do) for transport if the taxis for the clients ¹⁴_____ (not / arrive)?

c. If the delivery ¹⁵_____ (get) there late, the customer ¹⁶_____ (not / be) very happy.

d. If a lot of people ¹⁷_____ (accept) the invitation, we ¹⁸_____ (have to) find a new venue.

e. What ¹⁹_____ (your boss / think) if all the staff ²⁰_____ (ask) for a pay-rise?

Business communication

Jose visits your factory from Portugal. Write appropriate sentences.

21. Invite Jose for a drink after work.
    _____

22. Jose needs help with his laptop. Offer to help.
    _____

23. Offer Jose a cup of tea.
    _____

24. Jose invites you to the theatre this evening. Decline and give a reason.
    _____

25. Invite Jose to your house for dinner.
    _____

26. Jose offers you a bottle of Portuguese wine. Accept politely.
    _____

27. Jose invites you out to lunch today. You prefer to go tomorrow.
    _____

28. Jose needs to do some interviewing while he is with you. Offer Jose the use of your office.
    _____

29. Jose invites you to visit him in Lisbon. Accept.
    _____

30. Jose needs to write a report on his visit. Offer to help him with it.
    _____

Result _____ / 30 marks

Speaking test

Unit 11 | Tests

Role cards

Copy this page and cut out the role cards for the students. Then use the *Speaking test results* forms to evaluate each student's performance. You can then cut out the results and give them to the students.

Cut along this line

Student A

You and Student B are going to take out Lucy Eales, an important visitor from the USA, to dinner tonight. You have to decide where to take her and who is going to do various tasks connected with the visit.

You would like to go to *Il Pasto*, a cheap but excellent Italian restaurant near the office. Your colleague would like to go to *The Dining Room*, a very expensive Thai restaurant in a nearby town.

- Decide together which restaurant to go to and at what time – you prefer early.
- Talk about what will happen if you go to one of the restaurants.
- Invite the other person for a drink at your house beforehand.
- Offer to pick up Lucy from her hotel.

Student B

You and Student A are going to take out Lucy Eales, an important visitor from the USA, to dinner tonight. You have to decide where to take her and who is going to do various tasks connected with the visit.

You would like to go to *The Dining Room*, a very expensive Thai restaurant in a nearby town. Your colleague would like to go to *Il Pasto*, a cheap but excellent Italian restaurant near the office.

- Decide together which restaurant to go to and at what time – you prefer late.
- Talk about what will happen if you go to one of the restaurants.
- Invite the other person for a drink at the pub after the meal.
- Offer to book a table at the restaurant.

Cut along this line

Speaking test results

Use these forms to evaluate the students.

Cut along this line

Student A

Can the student …	Didn't do this (0 points)	Yes, but with some mistakes (1 point)	Yes, did this very well (2 points)
talk about future possibilities?			
invite somebody to do something?			
offer to do something?			
accept or decline an invitation / offer?			
come to a decision with somebody?			

Result _____ / 10 marks

Student B

Can the student …	Didn't do this (0 points)	Yes, but with some mistakes (1 point)	Yes, did this very well (2 points)
talk about future possibilities?			
invite somebody to do something?			
offer to do something?			
accept or decline an invitation / offer?			
come to a decision with somebody?			

Result _____ / 10 marks

Cut along this line

Photocopiable © Oxford University Press

12 | Progress test

Working with words

Complete these words with the missing letters.

1 It's very en_____ that our profits have risen so much.
2 This company has a re_____ for good management.
3 You can't say you have a high di_____ of your workforce when all the managers are men!
4 Our share price is sa_____, but it could be a lot higher.
5 TGG has a good sa_____ record, with only one accident in two years.
6 This firm is going to be the most socially re_____ organization in the country.
7 The CEO said our results were good, but I thought they were di_____.
8 The only way we can ac_____ our targets is by working extra hard.
9 Environmental pe_____ is increasingly important in modern business life.
10 We have taken various initiatives to manage co_____.

Language at work

A journalist interviews Dr Hai Hong about her new job at British Biotube. Complete the interview with the correct form of the verb in brackets, present perfect, or past simple.

J Well, Dr Hong, how long [11]_____ (you / work) at British Biotube now?
H Just two weeks. I [12]_____ (arrive) in the UK in June.
J Where [13]_____ (you / work) before that?
H Well, I [14]_____ (graduate) from Beijing University in 2006. Then I [15]_____ (spend) three years in the USA.
J Why [16]_____ (you / decide) to come to the UK?
H Well, I [17]_____ (want) to work here all my life! And my husband [18]_____ (be) here for two years now. He's working as a surgeon in York.
J What's the biggest problem you [19]_____ (find) since you came here?
H The language. People here speak very fast!
J How long [20]_____ (you / study) English at school?
H Six years. But that was a long time ago …

Business communication

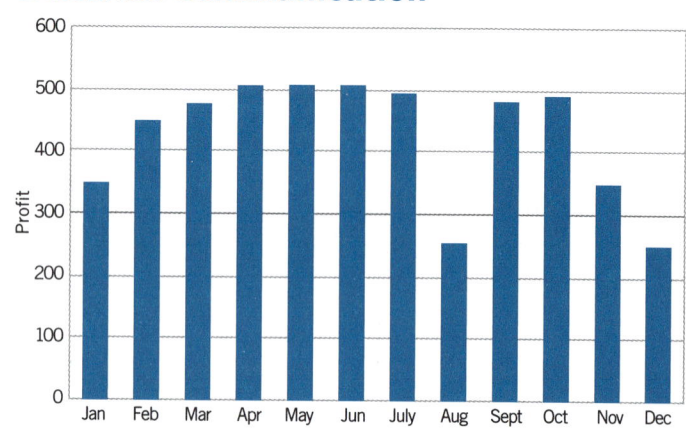

Complete the description of the graph with five *different* verbs.

Profits in January were €350,000 but [21]_____ in the next months to just over €450,000 in April. They [22]_____ stable from April to July, but then [23]_____ sharply between July and August as the summer holidays hit sales. Profits [24]_____ to nearly €500,000 in September and October, but then [25]_____ through November and December to reach €250,000 by the end of the year.

Complete the sentences with a preposition from the list.

at	by	from	to	to

26 Average salaries rose _____ 2.4% last year.
27/ 28 The salary of a typical office worker in London rose _____ £24,000 in January _____ about £24,500 by the end of the twelve months.
29 The price of a three-bedroomed house finished the year _____ £475,000.
30 Shares in TKG Houses fell about 5% _____ 475p in December.

Result _____ / 30 marks

Speaking test

Role cards

Copy this page and cut out the role cards for the students. Then use the *Speaking test results* forms to evaluate each student's performance. You can then cut out the results and give them to the students.

Cut along this line

Student A

You have worked for a house building company for a year. Your company is doing really well (see below) and you have just received a large bonus. However, there have been several accidents on your company's projects which have been in the newspapers, and which have damaged its reputation.

You meet the other person at a conference.

- Introduce yourself and your company. Find out how long they have been in the job.
- Find out how their company is doing in terms of sales, profit, and other aspects of performance.
- Give approximate information about your own company.

Your company this year:

- sales up 57.4%
- profits up 22.309%
- number of employees: 598
- accidents: six in last year, three serious

Student B

You have worked for a furniture company for three years. Your company is doing poorly (see below) and some employees have lost their jobs. However, the company has received a prize as 'Greenest Local Company' which was in the newspapers, and which has improved its reputation.

You meet the other person at a conference.

- Introduce yourself and your company. Find out how long they have been in the job.
- Find out how their company is doing in terms of sales, profit, and other aspects of performance.
- Give approximate information about your own company.

Your company this year:

- sales down 0.04%
- profits down 6.5%
- number of employees: 245, down from 300 last year
- accidents: none

Cut along this line

Speaking test results

Use these forms to evaluate the students.

Cut along this line

Student A

Can the student …	Didn't do this (0 points)	Yes, but with some mistakes (1 point)	Yes, did this very well (2 points)
ask and talk about how long you have worked for your company?			
ask about company performance?			
describe company performance?			
use figures accurately?			
use approximations?			

Result _____ / 10 marks

Student B

Can the student …	Didn't do this (0 points)	Yes, but with some mistakes (1 point)	Yes, did this very well (2 points)
ask and talk about how long you have worked for your company?			
ask about company performance?			
describe company performance?			
use figures accurately?			
use approximations?			

Result _____ / 10 marks

Cut along this line

Photocopiable © Oxford University Press

13 | Progress test

Working with words

Complete the sentences with words from the list. Change the form of the word if necessary.

issue	deteriorate	forecast	supply	run
improve	demand	growth	shortage	
estimate	renewable	development		

1 Most experts _____ that oil will become more expensive in the future.

2 Population _____ will mean that by the year 2020, there will be 30% more people in the world.

3 In desert areas, there is often a water _____.

4 I don't think we will ever _____ out of oil.

5 The situation has _____ badly since last year – we are much worse off.

6 We need to find some sources of _____ energy before it is too late.

7 World _____ of minerals like copper is starting to dry up.

8 Everybody needs oil, so _____ for it is likely to go up.

9 Our sales department has _____ that sales will rise 10% next year.

10 If the market doesn't _____ soon, we'll have big problems.

11 Economic _____ in India means that more people want to buy cars.

12 The search for water has become a global _____.

Language at work

Re-write the sentences using the verb in brackets.

13 I am sure people are going to work more. (will)

People _____

14 Some people say our desks will look different in ten years' time. (might)

Our desks _____

15 It is possible that oil will not run out. (may)

Oil _____

16 People are sure to want to work even in the future. (will)

People _____

Answer the questions using the words.

17 What will happen? I think / may / a lot of problems.
_____

18 What do you think of the oil crisis? I'm relaxed about it. I / sure / will / enough oil / many years.
_____

19 Is there a meeting on Friday? We don't know yet. The HR manager is ill, so / might not / be a meeting.
_____

20 What's your forecast for the share price? I'm very confident about it. It / not / fall.
_____

Business communication

Choose the correct answer from the words in *italics*.

21 Is your company *likely / hopeful* to do well next year?

22 *Do you think / Are you thinking* the climate situation will get better or worse?

23 Many people *is / are* likely to lose their jobs.

24 *Hopefully / Likely*, this scheme will save us money.

25 Governments are unlikely *to make / making* a decision soon.

26 Prices *won't probably / probably won't* go up much.

27 The new members of staff *may / will* definitely be unhappy about this.

28 Teleworking is *unlikely / definite* to change my life.

29 Companies like Apple *are likely to / will likely* do well in the current climate.

30 We will *definite / definitely* need to be greener.

Result _____ / 30 marks

Speaking test

Role cards

Copy this page and cut out the role cards for the students. Then use the *Speaking test results* forms to evaluate each student's performance. You can then cut out the results and give them to the students.

Cut along this line

Student A

You and Student B both work for a small company in Brussels which provides translation services to the EU. You have about 30 employees. You have heard a rumour that the CEO is planning to reduce the number of employees to save money, and relocate to another European city. You think the rumours are untrue because:

- translation services are always needed
- relocating would be a bad idea – Brussels is the perfect place for such a company
- the company made a lot of money last year.

Ask the other person what they think will happen to your company in the future. Say what you think may or will happen and what your hopes are.

Student B

You and Student A both work for a small company in Brussels which provides translation services to the EU. You have about 30 employees. You have heard a rumour that the CEO is planning to reduce the number of employees to save money, and relocate to another European city. You think the rumours are true because:

- there are many companies offering the same service
- relocating would be a good idea – Brussels is an expensive place for a company and a lot of translation is done online anyway
- the company's order book for next year is not too healthy.

Ask the other person what they think will happen to your company in the future. Say what you think may or will happen and what your hopes are.

Cut along this line

Speaking test results

Use these forms to evaluate the students.

Cut along this line

Student A

Can the student …	Didn't do this (0 points)	Yes, but with some mistakes (1 point)	Yes, did this very well (2 points)
ask for a prediction?			
talk about what may happen?			
express certainty about what will happen?			
express their hopes?			
respond to the other person's forecasts and hopes?			

Result _____ / 10 marks

Student B

Can the student …	Didn't do this (0 points)	Yes, but with some mistakes (1 point)	Yes, did this very well (2 points)
ask for a prediction?			
talk about what may happen?			
express certainty about what will happen?			
express their hopes?			
respond to the other person's forecasts and hopes?			

Result _____ / 10 marks

Cut along this line

Unit 13 | Tests

Photocopiable © Oxford University Press

14 | Progress test

Working with words

Complete the email.

Hi Katie
I've been thinking about the meeting next Friday. People are coming from a long way for it, so I really don't want to ¹_____ a lot of time. First of all, I think it must start ²_____ time. It's scheduled for 9 a.m., and it should start at 9 a.m.! I don't think we have ³_____ time to talk about salaries. We have to keep focused on the project and whether we can ⁴_____ the deadline or not. We'll need to ⁵_____ at least two hours talking about this – say until 11 a.m. Then we can have a break of, say, fifteen minutes, which will ⁶_____ people time to have a chat and catch up on news. After the break we can ⁷_____ a bit of time by asking the participants to restrict their presentations to five minutes each maximum. I haven't had time to think about the second day. Could you plan a ⁸_____ for this? If one day is not long ⁹_____ to fit in everything, maybe we could think about a third day? Let's hope we have ¹⁰_____ to discuss all the points on the agenda.
Enrique

Language at work

Correct the mistakes.

11 If you could to visit any country, which would you choose?

12 Would it be acceptable for you to pay more if we are improved the quality?

13 What would you saying if I offered you promotion?

14 If you were able to change something about your job, what will it be?

15 The staff didn't be happy if we took away the water cooler.

16 If we wouldn't have such high costs on this project, we could make a large profit.

17 Would you work better if you have a faster computer?

18 If my boss has been a bit more flexible, I could take a holiday next week.

19 Many workers would benefit if they could took a few months off for a course.

20 This would be a great place for a holiday if there wasn't so many mosquitoes.

Business communication

Complete the conversation.

Dirk   Hi, Rosa. I'm afraid we have a ²¹p_____ with the order.

Rosa   Oh dear. What seems to be wrong ²²e_____?

Dirk   Well, ²³b_____, we ordered 2,000 brochures, but you've only sent 1,000.

Rosa   Really? Oh no. Well, would it be OK ²⁴i_____ we delivered the other 1,000 next Monday?

Dirk   I'm afraid that wouldn't be ²⁵a_____. We need them on Thursday for a trade fair.

Rosa   ²⁶W_____ if we sent them by express courier? That would ²⁷a_____ us to get them to you within a day.

Dirk   Yes, that would be ²⁸p_____ .

Rosa   But would you ²⁹a_____ to pay for some of the courier costs?

Dirk   Yes, I think we ³⁰c_____ do that. How about 50–50?

Result _____ / 30 marks

Speaking test

Role cards

Copy this page and cut out the role cards for the students. Then use the *Speaking test results* forms to evaluate each student's performance. You can then cut out the results and give them to the students.

Cut along this line

Student A

You run a chain of coffee shops. Student B supplies you with the coffee machines. A few weeks ago, you ordered ten coffee machines from Student B at €700 each to be delivered by the end of next month. Now you have found that you can buy the machines from another company for less. You ring him / her to negotiate a new price and deadline for this order. For you the price is extremely important, the deadline less so.

- Introduce and describe your problem with the order.
- Say what you would like to do about the price.
- Respond to the other person's suggestion.
- Make another offer.
- Come to an agreement on both price and deadline.

Student B

You supply coffee machines to coffee shops. Student A runs a chain of coffee shops. A few weeks ago, he / she ordered ten coffee machines at €700 each to be delivered by the end of next month. He / she rings you to make changes to the order. For you the price is quite important, so you don't want to make much reduction, but the deadline is very important for you as you have received another big order to be completed urgently. You would like to move Student A's deadline back by two or three months.

- Listen to Student A's problem and respond.
- Say what you would like to do about the price.
- Respond to the other person's second suggestion.
- Explain your problem about the deadline and say that you would like to change it.
- Come to an agreement on both price and deadline.

Cut along this line

Speaking test results

Use these forms to evaluate the students.

Cut along this line

Student A

Can the student …	Didn't do this (0 points)	Yes, but with some mistakes (1 point)	Yes, did this very well (2 points)
explain a problem they have with an order?			
make a suggestion or offer?			
respond to an offer?			
talk about times and deadlines?			
come to an agreement?			

Result _____ / 10 marks

Student B

Can the student …	Didn't do this (0 points)	Yes, but with some mistakes (1 point)	Yes, did this very well (2 points)
explain a problem they have with an order?			
make a suggestion or offer?			
respond to an offer?			
talk about times and deadlines?			
come to an agreement?			

Result _____ / 10 marks

Cut along this line

Photocopiable © Oxford University Press

15 | Progress test

Working with words

Write the phrase after the definition.

1 Tell the employee information about their performance and progress _____ _____

2 Have a better chance of moving up within the company _____ your _____ _____

3 An interview with your boss each year to check progress _____ _____

4 Give an employee the desire to do something _____

5 To give yourself objectives _____ your _____

6 To look at your job calmly and objectively _____ a _____ _____

7 Not letting your job keep you from your family _____ _____

8 Be successful in reaching your objectives _____ your _____

9 Do the job better _____ your _____

10 Learn how to do something better _____ _____

Language at work

Complete the email with the correct form of the verbs in the list.

| could x2   have to   must   mustn't   should   shouldn't x2 |

Dear Jim,

You asked me for some advice about your interview next week with Terry Alderson in Marketing. The main thing is that you 11_____ be late. He's really big on punctuality. In fact, you 12_____ get there at least fifteen minutes early. Terry's not a formal kind of guy, so you 13_____ wear a suit – jacket and tie is fine. But you 14_____ be neat and clean-looking – Terry thinks that's really important in marketing.

He always likes somebody with the personal touch, so you 15_____ ask him about his family. But you 16_____ ask too many personal questions, because he'll get bored.

There are some questions he 17_____ ask you by law – things like your criminal record, etc. That's normal – don't worry about it. It'll be a long interview – maybe two hours or more. You 18_____ ask for a break in the middle – that might be a good idea.

Hope this helps,
Gianni

Business communication

Complete the conversation.

Dan   Natalia has just told me she's not happy with my work.

Alina   I 19_____. Did she say why?

Dan   No.

Alina   Don't 20_____. She's just stressed out at the moment.

Dan   But she says something like this every day.

Alina   I know 21_____ you feel. She's the same with me. It's not your 22_____. Have you 23_____ of doing yoga?

Dan   Yoga? Because my boss hates me? I 24_____ do that.

Alina   Look, Dan, I 25_____ totally, but really you shouldn't think too much about it. Why 26_____ you go for a coffee and relax?

Dan   Yes, good 27_____. I hope she isn't in the canteen!

Alina   She has a deadline today. Perhaps you 28_____ wait until next week and then ask if you can talk to her.

Dan   Yes, that might be 29_____.

Alina   I'm sure there's a 30_____. It's just a question of timing.

Result _____ / 30 marks

116   Photocopiable © Oxford University Press

Speaking test

Role card

This *Speaking test* has only one role card because each student has to give an individual presentation. Copy this page and cut out the role card for the student. Then use the *Speaking test results* forms to evaluate each student's performance. You can then cut out the results and give them to the student.

Cut along this line

Prepare and give a mini-presentation. Follow these stages:

- Introduce and describe briefly the place where you work.
- Describe what programmes (if any) are in place for the staff's personal development.
- Describe how much you have used them and what benefits you received.
- Suggest improvements which could be made, and which new programmes should be introduced.
- Thank the audience for their attention.

Cut along this line

Speaking test results

Use this form to evaluate the student.

Cut along this line

Can the student …	Didn't do this (0 points)	Yes, but with some mistakes (1 point)	Yes, did this very well (2 points)
describe their place of work?			
describe the company's personal development programmes?			
say how he / she used them?			
suggest improvements and new programmes?			
thank the audience appropriately?			

Result _____ / 10 marks

Cut along this line

Photocopiable © Oxford University Press

Unit 15 | Tests

16 | Progress test

Working with words

Complete the profile with words from the list. Change the form of the word if necessary.

ambition	challenge	change	weakness
strength	concentrate	decision	give up
path	spend	complete

Lee Jae Kyun [1]_____ his degree in physics at York University in 1998. After that he [2]_____ three years working for a biotechnology company near London, and his career [3]_____ seemed to be mapped out. But in 2001 he [4]_____ this position, and made the [5]_____ to move to the USA to [6]_____ on an academic career. Undoubtedly he is one the most brilliant students I have ever taught. His main [7]_____ is that he is able to make links between different parts of the same discipline. His only [8]_____ is that he finds a lot of the work very easy, and starts to become lazy. We hope this does not mean that he will [9]_____ jobs every two years because he gets bored, and wants a new [10]_____. He says his [11]_____ is to run a major laboratory in an American or European scientific organization.

Language at work

Put the verbs in brackets in the correct tense.

12 Recently, I _____ (work) on a big contract with Sony.

13 At the moment, we _____ (look) at ways of reducing costs.

14 If you _____ (not / like) the decision, you'll find a lot of people who disagree with you.

15 You _____ (not / smoke) in this area of the factory.

16 If we _____ (have) more cash, we would be able to spend more money on the restaurant facilities.

17 From 2003 to 2007, Maribel _____ (be) the CEO of a big South American company.

18 A lorry _____ (arrive) every week from Poland with spare parts.

19 This company was _____ (start) up in 1947.

20 Every employee _____ (have) to wear a uniform with the company logo on the front.

Business communication

In each sentence of the presentation, there is a mistake with the time phrase or the verb form. Correct the mistakes.

21 Hi. My name's David Torres, and I'm with the company since 2004.

22 The last year I was promoted to Sales Manager.

23 Recently, I've meeting most of the sales reps …

24 … and I meet the others over the next twelve months.

25 At the moment, the company goes through a difficult time …

26 … but I am sure that in a future, this situation will improve.

27 From 2005 to 2007, profits have risen by over 10% every year …

28 … and on my current role, I am looking forward to reaching similar targets again.

29 Up to now, I listen hard to my staff …

30 … and I going to continue to do so.

Result _____ / 30 marks

118

Speaking test

Role cards

This *Speaking test* has only one role card because students work together. Copy this page and cut out the role card for pairs of students. Then use the *Speaking test results* forms to evaluate each student's performance. You can then cut out the results and give them to the student.

Cut along this line

Work in pairs

You are careers advisors. You have been asked to provide careers advice for Jeff Machado, who would like to change careers. Read the notes about Jeff.

Jeff Machado, aged 24

Qualifications: Vocational Qualification in Preparing and Serving Food

Current situation: one of 60 chefs working in the main kitchen of EatPlus, a large catering company which supplies food and drink to schools and colleges. Has worked there for five years since he qualified.

Interests: Painting, graphics, music, sport

Strengths: Intelligent, creative, energetic, very hard-working when interested

Weaknesses: Lazy when bored, not very academic

Ambitions: unsure – maybe something in music and / or graphic arts. Probably not in catering, where he is getting frustrated with the routine and low pay.

Discuss Jeff's case, and suggest a new career path for him.
- Review Jeff's career so far.
- Describe his current position and why it is unsatisfactory for him.
- Suggest a new career path.
- Agree to meet on a specified day and time to write report for Jeff.
- Say goodbye.

Cut along this line

Speaking test results

Use this form to evaluate the student.

Cut along this line

Student A

Can the student …	Didn't do this (0 points)	Yes, but with some mistakes (1 point)	Yes, did this very well (2 points)
describe someone's career so far?			
describe their current situation?			
suggest a new career path with reasons?			
agree to meet on a specified day and time?			
say goodbye appropriately?			

Result _____ / 10 marks

Student B

Can the student …	Didn't do this (0 points)	Yes, but with some mistakes (1 point)	Yes, did this very well (2 points)
describe someone's career so far?			
describe their current situation?			
suggest a new career path with reasons?			
agree to meet on a specified day and time?			
say goodbye appropriately?			

Result _____ / 10 marks

Cut along this line

Photocopiable © Oxford University Press

DVD worksheet | Intercultural communication

Material used in the DVD

Business Result Pre-intermediate Student's Book, Unit 6, page 39.

Part 1 | How can cultural differences affect communication?

1 Complete these tables with cultural facts about your own nationality / culture and another nationality / culture you know well. Then consider how similar / different the two cultures are and whether any differences could affect communication.

Your culture
Ways of greeting / body language and gesture:
Level of politeness or formality:
Attitudes towards time:
Topics or behaviour that are taboo:
Importance of small talk and relationship building before working together:
Being direct or indirect:

Another culture
Ways of greeting / body language and gesture:
Level of politeness or formality:
Attitudes towards time:
Topics or behaviour that are taboo:
Importance of small talk and relationship building before working together:
Being direct or indirect:

2 ▶ Watch this section and answer questions 1–3.

1 Which of the factors in the tables above are mentioned by the students and author in this section of the DVD? Make notes on what they say.

_____

_____

2 What is the main topic of the lesson? How does the teacher connect the topic to cultural differences?

_____

Photocopiable © Oxford University Press

3 David (the co-author) describes two different types of culture. What are they?
_____

4 At the end of this section, how does Geraldine (the French student) define her company's culture? What does the company have to 'balance'?
_____

Part 2 | How can we approach cultural training in the classroom?

3 Which of the following approaches to teaching culture would be appropriate in the business English classroom? How might the specific needs of your students affect your choice?
   a Give students a lecture about how to behave in your country.
   b Ask students what they have noticed about communicating with different nationalities and how this affects the language they choose.
   c Give students a list of 'dos and don'ts' for dealing with people from different countries.
   d Ask students to compare the way their company does things with their partner's.

4 ▶ Watch this section. Based on what David says, which approaches in 3 do you think he would use in class?
_____

5 Judith (the teacher) is teaching language for complaining. Look at the following three stages of her lesson plan. She also includes two stages dealing with intercultural issues. What does she do during these stages and when does she include them?
   a Play a listening of some situations with complaints
   b Drill the expressions for intonation
   c Provide role-play practice with the new language

6 How could you integrate the topic of cultural similarities and differences into the following four business English teaching situations? What issues might arise in each situation?

   Situation 1: The teacher is introducing the language of meeting and greeting people at a conference.
   _____

   Situation 2: The students are going to do some role-plays involving negotiations over the phone between a customer and a supplier.
   _____

   Situation 3: The students are going to write letters as if their company is introducing its products to a potential client on another continent.
   _____

   Situation 4: The aim of the lesson is to provide language for describing rules and codes of behaviour in companies. By the end of the lesson students will give presentations on company policies as if speaking to a group of new employees from different countries.
   _____

Photocopiable © Oxford University Press

DVD worksheet | Intercultural communication

DVD worksheet | Meetings

Material used in the DVD
Business Result Pre-intermediate Student's Book, Unit 6, page 40.

Part 1 | What types of meetings do students attend?

1 Think of a meeting you recently attended either for work (e.g. a teachers' meeting, meeting a colleague to discuss a student), or in your free time (e.g. a society or committee) and answer questions 1–3.
   1 Was the meeting formal or informal?
   2 Was it planned or unplanned?
   3 Was it face to face or via the Internet / phone?

2 During your meeting do you remember doing any of the following? What did you say? Think of one expression for each function.
   Giving an opinion: _____
   Asking for an opinion: _____
   Interrupting: _____
   Agreeing: _____
   Disagreeing: _____
   Suggesting: _____

3 If you already teach business English students, what kinds of meetings do they attend?
   _____

4 ▶ Watch this section and answer questions 1–3.
   1 What kinds of meetings did Burcu Akbaba attend for her company?
   _____

   2 What are the two kinds of meetings that David (the co-author) describes?
   _____

   3 Which of the functions listed in **2** is Judith (the teacher) working on with her pre-intermediate class?
   _____

Part 2 | What do students find difficult about meetings?

5 Read this list of difficulties students often face when participating in meetings in English. Have you or your students ever experienced these difficulties during a meeting?

1 Meetings with native speakers: Many students find it easier to have meetings with other non-native speakers – dealing with native speakers is often much harder.
2 Different conventions: Both national and company cultures will affect how meetings are run (e.g. some will follow an agenda point by point whilst others may move around or discuss items that are not on the agenda).
3 Preparation beforehand: Non-native speakers in particular benefit from receiving information on the topics of the meeting so that they can prepare what they need to say. Impromptu meetings may be more difficult.

4 Turn-taking: It's helpful to know when it's appropriate to interrupt and agree or disagree. Cultural differences may influence a student's decision (e.g. a Japanese student may be less likely to interrupt and disagree than someone from France).
5 Level of formality: The language we choose to use will be affected by the level of formality. Students need to recognize how formal the meeting is and what language is needed.
6 Can the participants see each other? With conference calls, students may have the added difficulty of not being able to see the other participants.

6 ▶ Watch this section and answer questions 1–2.

1 Which difficulty in **5** does David refer to and which does Burcu refer to?

___

2 Do you think the activity with the expressions on paper will help with either of the difficulties mentioned by David or Burcu? What other classroom activities might help with the difficulties in **5**?

___

Part 3 | How can we approach teaching meetings?

7 There are several different ways to set up a simulation for a meeting. What would be the pros and cons of the following two approaches?

Approach A: Provide the agenda and give the students information on and background to the meeting. Each student can have a role card with an assigned view or opinion.

Approach B: Elicit an agenda from the students that relates to their own work or background in some way.

___

___

8 ▶ Watch this section and answer questions 1–4.

1 Which approach does Judith seem to prefer in this lesson? What are her reasons?

___

2 Once the students begin their meeting, listen carefully to their language. Did the students use expressions that had been taught earlier in the lesson?

___

3 Did they use any other functional language that seemed to be useful?

___

4 How well did the students seem to be achieving the task?

___

9 In her interview about the final meeting simulation, Judith says:

> ❝In the final meeting this afternoon they did start off by using the phrases and language that we'd practised, but as the meeting progressed the fluency increased and the task took over from the language.❞

Do you think it is a problem that the students stopped using the target language from the earlier part of the lesson? Does it need to be resolved?

Photocopiable © Oxford University Press

DVD worksheet | Self-study

Material used in the DVD

Business Result Pre-intermediate Student's Book, Practice files.
Business Result Interactive Workbook on CD-ROM
Business Result student's website, www.oup.com/elt/result

Part 1 | How do you study on your own?

1 Think about when you have studied another language. Tick [✓] the techniques listed in the table that you have used for self-study. Which were particularly successful for you?

	You	Your students	Burcu	Kevser	Geraldine
do exercises in a text book / grammar book					
watch TV / films / DVDs					
listen to the radio / audio / downloads					
speak the language with other people					
write to other people in the language					
read newspapers / books / Internet					
other?					

2 Now think about your students. Tick [✓] the self-study strategies that they use.

3 ▶ Watch this section. Listen to three students talking about how they study on their own. Tick [✓] the strategies that they use.

Part 2 | How much time do you have for self-study?

4 How much time per week do you think your students spend studying on their own?

_____

5 Do they always do their homework or is it difficult for them to find time to study?

_____

6 ▶ Watch this section and answer questions 1–2.

1 What are the reasons given by the two business English students for not having enough time to study? Are these similar to the reasons your students give?

_____
_____

2 Why does David (the co-author) think we shouldn't always be concerned about business English students' lack of time for self-study?

_____

Part 3 | How can teachers help with self-study?

7 Look at this list of tips and ideas for helping students with self-study. Which ones do you suggest to your students? Do you have any other techniques?

- establish from the beginning of the course how much time they will realistically have for self-study
- develop a timetable or schedule blocks of time in their diary for self-study periods
- advise them to listen to CDs or downloads while waiting in traffic on their way to work
- show them how to make use of the Internet or computer-based software for self-study
- set realistic amounts of homework (not too much) for the time they have
- find out what the students will be doing at work over the week and how much they are likely to be using English in their work
- make use of self-study materials provided with a course book
- try to incorporate study tasks into their work; for example, if they are writing emails, give them expressions to use and ask them to bring in copies of the emails to class
- be consistent in checking homework and giving feedback so students feel that self-study is as important as classroom study

8 ▶ Watch this section and answer questions 1–3.

1 Which of the techniques in **7** are mentioned by David and Cathy (the teacher)?

_____

2 Which three features of *Business Result* are useful for self-study?

_____

3 Cathy explains to a student how to use the Interactive Workbook for self-study.
   a What can students do with the sample emails?

   _____

   b What can students listen to?

   _____

   c What features does the glossary contain?

   _____

Photocopiable © Oxford University Press

Progress test answer key

Unit 1

1. specialize
2. competitors
3. employees
4. based
5. sales
6. do
7. Why
8. Does
9. is
10. many
11. 9
12. 6
13. 10
14. 8
15. 7
16. Could you ~~to~~ speak more clearly?
17. **Could** I have a glass of water, please?
18. Can you **give** me your address?
19. Yes, of course ~~not~~.
20. Can you **lend** me your mobile?
21. e
22. b
23. g
24. i
25. c
26. h
27. d
28. f
29. a
30. j

Unit 2

1. I'm not involved in talking to customers.
2. Sarah deals with software issues.
3. My job consists of telephoning suppliers.
4. Do you ever take part in meetings and discussions with subcontractors?
5. Peter's work involves organizing travel for his colleagues.
6. employment agency
7. customer
8. public relations officer
9. subcontractors
10. colleague
11. supplier
12. consultant
13. is working
14. does your company work
15. 'm expecting
16. Are you working
17. uses
18. is thinking
19. 'm just leaving
20. doesn't involve
21. speak
22. phoning/calling
23. This
24. about
25. calling/phoning
26. afraid
27. leave
28. course
29. back
30. welcome

Unit 3

1. IT
2. Human Resources
3. Purchasing
4. Training
5. Logistics
6. Quality Control
7. Technical Support
8. Research and Development
9. Finance
10. Marketing
11. Which department do you work in?
12. How many people does your company employ?
13. What are you working on at the moment?
14. Which do you prefer, tea or coffee?
15. How often do you visit Japan?
16. Where does he come from?
17. How long are you staying?
18. When did you / your company move here?
19. How much do you know about the Australian market?
20. What does your company produce?
21. i
22. c
23. f
24. j
25. b
26. d
27. g
28. a
29. e
30. h

Unit 4

1. idea
2. compact
3. did
4. well
5. cheap
6. designed
7. trials
8. stylish
9. launched
10. friendly
11. Felipe didn't go to Paris yesterday.
12. Did you see the new consultants last week?
13. I didn't receive your letter.
14. The sales team met the new director this morning.
15. Did the product have any success at the conference?
16. We didn't **find** the presentation very interesting.
17. The company **bought** a lot of new furniture.
18. Francesca **didn't / did not enjoy** the meal with the sales manager.
19. They **arrived** at the airport at 6 p.m. yesterday.
20. The report **wasn't** very informative.
21. e
22. b
23. h
24. a
25. f
26. j
27. i
28. c
29. g
30. d

Unit 5

1. bonus
2. update
3. shortlist
4. leave
5. subsidized
6. form
7. scheme
8. position
9. hours
10. advertisement
11. Have you applied for the job yet?
12. I have already sent my CV to the company.
13. They didn't get any paid holiday last year.
14. Has she been to France this month?
15. When did you leave your last job?
16. Where are we
17. running out
18. Have you done
19. short of time
20. deal with it
21. leave it to
22. what about
23. I talked
24. Has he
25. I haven't

Unit 6

1. meet
2. keep
3. on time
4. deal
5. back
6. encourage
7. conducted
8. satisfied
9. personalized
10. provide
11. This is the **best** restaurant in town.
12. The job was not as **easy** as we expected.
13. Marcia's **the** most hard-working employee in this company.
14. Our sales figures are the **lowest** they've been for twenty years.
15. Our rival BJT has the **biggest** market share.

16. Market conditions are more **difficult** than last year.
17. The **least** profitable of our three divisions is Europe.
18. We need to think of ways of making our staff **happier**.
19. Can you be **more careful** in future?
20. The new building is **better** than the old one in many ways.
21. What do you think about that?
22. Personally, I feel / think
23. I don't agree at all.
24. I agree with you.
25. I think you're right.

Unit 7

1. trip
2. flight
3. delayed
4. terminal
5. checked
6. bill
7. gate
8. departure
9. boarded
10. luggage
11. key card
12. safe
13. one-way
14. shuttle
15. Is there a hotel near here?
16. How much luggage have you got?
17. How many times have you been to Beijing?
18. Are there (any) taxis at this time of night?
19. How much travelling do you do in a year?
20. Have we got (any / enough) time to do any shopping?
21. been
22. How
23. kind
24. did
25. go
26. trip
27. Did
28. on
29. Are
30. think

Unit 8

1. stock
2. place
3. delivered
4. invoice
5. track
6. purchased
7. gave
8. process
9. make
10. quote
11. complaint
12. Are you doing
13. 'm going to stay
14. are going
15. 's starting
16. 'll come
17. are you meeting
18. 'll bring
19. won't say
20. Shall
21. about
22. about
23. great
24. Let's
25. should
26. don't
27. could
28. think
29. suggest
30. should / could

Unit 9

1. entered
2. attract
3. campaign
4. mouth
5. boosted
6. share
7. launch
8. advertising
9. Direct
10. expand
11. have to / need to
12. can
13. have to / need to
14. aren't allowed to
15. can
16. aren't allowed

127

Progress test answer key

17 do I have
18 can
19 aren't allowed
20 don't need to/ don't have to / needn't
21 come back
22 move on
23 sum up
24 said
25 discuss
26 getting off
27 covered
28 Could
29 'm
30 catch

Unit 10

1 popular
2 friendly
3 initiative
4 convenient
5 value
6 unusual
7 recycled
8 effective
9 original
10 useful
11 were recycled
12 want
13 take
14 are collected
15 (are) transported
16 melts
17 is made
18 are bought
19 fill
20 are sold
21 I'll talk about that **later**.
22 That brings **me** to my next point.
23 First **of** all, I'd like to say a few words about recycling.
24 Thanks very much for **listening** today.
25 My next **point** is about company image.
26 As I **said** before, the problem is complicated.
27 I'm here today **to** tell you about the benefits of carbon offsetting.
28 Let's move **on** to my next point.
29 Good afternoon **everybody**.
30 We're going to **look** at the subject of carbon emissions.

Unit 11

1 event
2 venue
3 entertain
4 guests
5 booked
6 arranged
7 invitations
8 accept
9 purpose
10 reinforce
11 is
12 'll play
13 will you do
14 don't arrive
15 gets
16 won't/will not be
17 accept
18 have to
19 will your boss think
20 ask
21 Would you like to go for a drink after work?
22 Would you like me to help you with that?
23 Would you like a cup of tea?
24 Oh thank you for the invitation, but I'm afraid I'm busy.
25 Would you like to come to my house for dinner?
26 Oh thank you, that's very kind of you.
27 That would be nice, but I'd rather go tomorrow.
28 Would you like to use my office?
29 Oh yes, that would be great!
30 Shall I help you with it?

Unit 12

1 encouraging
2 reputation
3 diversity
4 satisfactory
5 safety
6 responsible
7 disappointing
8 achieve
9 performance
10 costs
11 have you been working / have you worked
12 arrived
13 did you work
14 graduated
15 spent
16 did you decide
17 have wanted
18 has been
19 have found
20 did you study
21 rose / increased
22 remained
23 fell
24 increased / rose
25 declined
26 by
27 from
28 to
29 at
30 to

Unit 13

1 forecast / estimate
2 growth
3 shortage
4 run
5 deteriorated
6 renewable
7 supply
8 demand
9 estimated / forecast
10 improve
11 development
12 issue
13 People will work more.
14 Our desks might look different in ten years' time.
15 Oil may not run out.
16 People will want to work even in the future.
17 I think there may be a lot of problems.
18 I'm sure there will be enough oil for many years.

19 … there might not be a meeting.
20 It won't fall.
21 likely
22 Do you think
23 are
24 Hopefully
25 to make
26 probably won't
27 will
28 unlikely
29 are likely to
30 definitely

Unit 14

1 waste
2 on
3 enough
4 meet
5 spend
6 give
7 save
8 schedule
9 enough
10 time
11 If you could ~~to~~ visit any country, which would you choose?
12 Would it be acceptable for you to pay more if we ~~are~~ improved the quality?
13 What would you **say** if I offered you promotion?
14 If you were able to change something about your job, what **would** it be?
15 The staff **wouldn't** be happy if we took away the water cooler.
16 If we **didn't** have such high costs on this project, we could make a large profit.
17 **Will** you work better if you have a faster computer? or Would you work better if you **had** a faster computer?
18 If my boss **was** a bit more flexible, I could take a holiday next week.
19 Many workers would benefit if they could **take** a few months off for a course.

20 This would be a great place for a holiday if there **weren't** so many mosquitoes.
21 problem
22 exactly
23 basically
24 if
25 acceptable
26 What
27 allow
28 possible
29 agree
30 could

Unit 15

1 give feedback
2 improve your promotion prospects
3 annual appraisal
4 motivate
5 set your goals
6 take a step back
7 work / life balance
8 achieve your goals
9 improve your performance
10 develop skills
11 mustn't
12 should
13 shouldn't
14 must
15 could
16 shouldn't
17 has to
18 could
19 see
20 worry
21 how
22 fault
23 thought
24 can't
25 understand
26 don't
27 idea
28 could
29 possible
30 solution

Unit 16

1 completed
2 spent
3 path
4 gave up
5 decision
6 concentrate
7 strength
8 weakness
9 change
10 challenge
11 ambition
12 have worked / have been working
13 are looking
14 don't like
15 shouldn't / aren't allowed to / mustn't smoke
16 had
17 was
18 arrives
19 started
20 has
21 Hi. My name's David Torres, and **I've been** with the company since 2004.
22 ~~The~~ Last year I was promoted to Sales Manager.
23 Recently, I've **been** meeting / **I've met** most of the sales reps …
24 … and **I'm going to** meet the others over the next twelve months.
25 At the moment, the company **is going** through a difficult time …
26 … but I am sure that in **the** future, this situation will improve.
27 From 2005 to 2007, profits **rose** by over 10% every year …
28 … and **in** my current role, I am looking forward to reaching similar targets again.
29 Up to now, I **have listened** hard to my staff …
30 … and **I'm** going to continue to do so.

Practice file answer key

Unit 1
Working with words
Exercise 1
2 f 3 e 4 b 5 c 6 a

Exercise 2
2 head
4 subsidiaries
6 sell
8 make
3 operate
5 employees
7 goods
9 competitors

Exercise 3
2 companies
4 goods
6 specialize
8 operates
10 produce
3 subsidiaries
5 based
7 provide
9 services

Business communication
Exercise 1
2 i 3 a 4 e 5 j 6 c
7 g 8 b 9 d 10 f

Language at work
Exercise 1
2 is   3 specialize   4 starts
5 works   6 start   7 have
8 specializes 9 are   10 work

Exercise 2
b does 5
d is 2
f are 9
h start 6
j does 8
c Do you have 7
e do 10
g does 1
i does 4

Exercise 3
2 don't
4 doesn't, does
6 don't
3 does
5 aren't

Unit 2
Working with words
Exercise 1
2 a training organization
3 a supplier
4 an employment agency
5 a subcontractor
6 a customer
7 a consultant

Exercise 2
2 e 3 a 4 b 5 c

Exercise 3
2 deal
4 take part
3 involves
5 consists

Business communication
Exercise 1
2 calling   3 This   4 afraid
5 take   6 ask   7 back
8 Does   9 give   10 help

Exercise 2
2 Yes, is that Seth speaking?
3 Are you phoning about that Japanese customer?
4 I'm calling to tell you that I'm sending them now.
5 Thanks very much for calling.
6 Speak to you later or maybe tomorrow.

Language at work
Exercise 1
2 Is he staying
3 You aren't / You're not listening
4 I'm leaving
5 are those German engineers visiting

Exercise 2
2 a 3 b 4 f 5 d 6 e

Exercise 3
2 have   3 work
4 are looking   5 buy
6 are becoming   7 are opening
8 get   9 are trying

Unit 3
Working with words
Exercise 1
2 c 3 g 4 e 5 f 6 h
7 j 8 a 9 b 10 i

Exercise 2
2 in charge of   3 reports to
4 for   5 with

Business communication
Exercise 1
2 a 3 c 4 a 5 c 6 b 7 a

Exercise 2
2 Can everybody see that OK?
3 As you can see
4 The important thing here is
5 Have a look at this table.
6 This table shows the breakdown of sales.

Language at work
Exercise 1
2 b 3 b 4 a 5 b 6 a
7 b 8 a 9 b 10 b

Exercise 2
2 When did the company start?
3 Where does it have its head office?
4 How many people does the company employ?
5 How much chewing gum do Americans eat?

Unit 4
Working with words
Exercise 1
2 market research
3 design
4 product trials
5 branded the product
6 launched

Exercise 2
Across:
6 convenient   7 stylish
8 well-designed
Down:
1 functional   2 user-friendly
3 compact   5 attractive

Business communication
Exercise 1
b 7
c 8
d 9
e 5
f 3
g 6
h 4
i 2

Exercise 2
2 We wanted
3 Why do we need
4 First
5 Then
6 We spoke to
7 Finally
8 We asked customers and staff
9 We found that

Language at work
Exercise 1
2 visited
3 met
4 took
5 had
6 did not / didn't finish
7 wanted
8 flew
9 made
10 did not / didn't go
11 went
12 interviewed
13 did not / didn't find

14 played
15 did not / didn't win
16 replied
17 wrote
18 attended
19 ended
20 did not / didn't get

Exercise 2
2 did you have lunch
3 did you see
4 did the manager leave
5 did they stay
6 did she join
7 did you spend
8 did you send

Unit 5
Working with words
Exercise 1
2 private healthcare
3 company car
4 pension scheme
5 subsidized childcare
6 gym membership
7 annual bonus
8 flexible hours
9 maternity leave
10 mobile phone

Exercise 2
2 application
3 Fill
4 CV
5 referees
6 position / post / job
7 interview
8 applicants

Business communication
Exercise 1
2 c 3 a 4 c 5 a

Exercise 2
b with   c Leave   d short
e Where   f already   g out
h about   i yet

Language at work
Exercise 1
2 have told
3 have not / haven't found
4 has become
5 has been
6 have already left
7 have not / haven't recruited
8 have / 've asked
9 has / e's said
10 have / 've lost
11 have not / haven't had
12 have not / haven't made

Exercise 2
2 Have you seen h
3 Have you ever a
4 Did you have d
5 Has c
6 Did g
7 Have you received b
8 Did you learn e

Unit 6
Working with words
Exercise 1
2 c 3 a 4 d 5 b 6 f

Exercise 2
2 meet the needs of customers
3 deal with complaints
4 encourage customer loyalty
5 offer a personalized service
6 get repeat business

Exercise 3
1 impossible   2 ✓
3 unhelpful   4 dissatisfied
5 ✓

Business communication
Exercise 1
2 Do, c   3 you're, a
4 should, d 5 I don't, f
6 How, e

Exercise 2
2 I don't agree at all.
3 I don't think
4 I agree
5 do you think
6 personally, I feel
7 I think you're right
8 do you feel

Language at work
Exercise 1
2 more profitable   3 largest
4 more expensive   5 better
6 most famous   7 the worst
8 the biggest

Exercise 2
2 ✓
3 The Edison Building is **the cheapest**.
4 The Soria Palace is **easier** to get to from the city centre than the Master Tower.
5 The Master Tower **is more modern than** the Soria Palace.
6 The Edison Building is the **smallest** of the three buildings.
7 The Soria Palace is **as expensive as** the Master Tower.
8 ✓

Unit 7
Working with words
Exercise 1
2 connection 3 leave   4 gate
5 reservation 6 facilities   7 luggage
8 board   9 delayed   10 safe

Exercise 2
2 d 3 g 4 h 5 a
6 f 7 i   8 c 9 e
2 departure lounge   3 key card
4 shuttle bus   5 double room
6 terminal building   7 one-way ticket
8 business trip   9 check-in desk

Business communication
Exercise 1
2 f 3 d 4 h 5 g
6 a 7 b 8 c

Exercise 2
2 been   3 often   4 go
5 see   6 Did   7 think
8 kind

Language at work
Exercise 1
Countable: flight, hotel, reservation, suitcase
Uncountable: information, luggage, money, travel, work

Exercise 2
2 is   3 is   4 many
5 some 6 is   7 much
8 was

Exercise 3
2 aren't 3 an   4 much
5 a   6 is   7 some
8 Are

Unit 8
Working with words
Exercise 1
2 a refund / some prices
3 an enquiry / a complaint
4 shipment / delivery
5 bill / invoice
6 order / price
7 goods / products

Exercise 2
1 deliver   2 order, check
3 make, track   4 confirm, quoted
5 make, ask for 6 cancel, ship
7 place, change 8 process, confirm

Business communication

Exercise 1
2 Maybe we should think about cancelling the order.
3 How about sending an email to Head Office?
4 Shall we talk about this again tomorrow?
5 We could advertise in the local newspaper.
6 I suggest we discuss this with the manager.

Exercise 2
b sure 2   c Let's 6   d think 5
e work 3   f Fine 4

Exercise 3
2 f   3 e   4 g   5 d   6 c   7 b

Language at work

Exercise 1
2 she's going to have   3 aren't going
4 I'm going to wash   5 he's visiting
6 won't be   7 I'm going to look
8 She's playing

Exercise 2
2 're not going to finish
3 'm meeting
4 'll ask
5 'm having
6 'll check
7 'm not going to get

Unit 9

Working with words

Exercise 1
2 offer   3 expand   4 launching
5 attracted   6 boost   7 enter
8 improved   9 discount   10 share

Exercise 2
2 outdoor advertising
3 TV advertisements
4 word-of-mouth
5 press ads
6 online adverts

Business communication

Exercise 1
2 c   3 a   4 b   5 f   6 h
7 i   8 j   9 e   10 g

Exercise 2
2 I didn't catch that.
3 I'm not with you.
4 Could you be more specific
5 What was that you said?
6 we're getting off the subject.
7 we can come back to that later.
8 we've covered everything
9 Can we move on to the next point
10 can we sum up what we've agreed

Language at work

Exercise 1
Students' own answers.

Exercise 2
2 Do I have
3 has to, are allowed
4 Am I allowed
5 need to
6 can, aren't allowed
7 don't have, can't

Unit 10

Working with words

Exercise 1
2 efficient   3 friendly   4 unusual
5 useful   6 initiative 7 recycling
8 convenient   9 original   10 value
11 affordable   12 disposal

Exercise 2
2 affordable
3 unusual
4 good value for money
5 recycling
6 convenient
7 initiative
8 efficient
9 popular

Business communication

Exercise 1
1 h   2 c   3 g   4 b   5 e
6 f   7 i   8 j   9 a   10 d

Exercise 2
2 I'm here today
3 I'll talk
4 First of all,
5 Let's move on
6 My next point
7 as I said before
8 That brings me
9 Thanks very much

Language at work

Exercise 1
2 The invoice **was** sent yesterday.
3 Over a thousand guests **were** invited to the event.
4 The post **is collected** at 10 a.m. every day.
5 The software is **written** by our own engineers.
6 The meeting was **cancelled** because of the strike.

Exercise 2
2 was first suggested
3 was published
4 saves
5 is often lost

Exercise 3
2 An email was sent by the HR department to all employees.
3 The money was stolen (by somebody) during the night.
4 The staff were informed by the Heads of Department about the decision.
5 Salaries are discussed with employees individually.
6 The key to the safe is kept (by him) in his desk.

Unit 11

Working with words

Exercise 1
2 event   3 venue   4 guests
5 budget   6 host company

Exercise 2
2 reinforce   3 arranged   4 entertains
5 booked   6 accept

Exercise 3
2 host company   3 entertain
4 purpose   5 reinforce
6 held   7 venue
8 accepted   9 budget
10 guests   11 book
12 arranged

Business communication

Exercise 1
2 Would you like to join us for lunch?
3 Shall I pick you up from the station?
4 Thanks but I'd rather get some sleep.
5 Would you like me to book a table?
6 Would you like a glass of water?
7 Thanks for the invitation but I'm not hungry.

Exercise 2
2 Would you like to stop for a break?
3 Would you like me to meet you at the airport?
4 Shall I get some tickets?
5 Would you like to visit the new factory now?

Exercise 3
2 Thanks for the   3 very kind of
4 like me to   5 thanks I'd rather
6 would be nice

Language at work

Exercise 1
2 is, won't
3 won't get, waits
4 don't hold, 'll lose
5 won't accept, doesn't like
6 arrange, won't arrive
7 'll cancel, rains

Exercise 2
2 If the singer is ill, they'll cancel the concert.
3 We won't go to the show if it finishes late.
4 How will they travel if the airline is on strike?
5 He'll call the host company if he doesn't receive an invitation.
6 What will you do if it snows on the day?
7 If she doesn't like the food, she'll order something different.

Exercise 3
2 isn't, 'll go
3 'll complain, runs out
4 continues, won't hold
5 won't find, don't give

Unit 12
Working with words

Exercise 1
2 f 3 h 4 a 5 g
6 c 7 b 8 d

Exercise 2
2 safety record, excellent
3 perform well, encouraging
4 satisfactory, socially responsible
5 poor, manage costs
6 environmental performance, satisfactory
7 diversity of the workforce, encouraging
8 good reputation, encouraging

Business communication

Exercise 1
2 from   3 to   4 by
5 to   6 by   7 to

Exercise 2
2 dropped   3 decreased
4 remained stable   5 risen
6 increasing

Exercise 3
Students' own answers

Language at work

Exercise 1
1 I **got** a degree from Portland University in 1998.
2 I **have worked** as a Manager at Portland Running Company since 2005.
3 I've been responsible for cost management **for** several years.
4 I **was** an Assistant Manager at One Step Fitness Club for three years.
5 At One Step Fitness Club I **developed** customer activities.
6 I **worked** as a sales assistant for four years.
7 I **left** One Step Fitness Club in 2005.

Exercise 2
2 When did she join One Step Fitness Club?
3 How long was she Assistant Manager at One Step Fitness Club?
4 How long has she been a manager?
5 Where did she work from 1998 to 2002?
6 How long has she been responsible for sales growth?
7 How long did she work at Sun Sports Clothing?
8 How long has she been in the sports and fitness industry?

Unit 13
Working with words

Exercise 1
2 world supply
3 economic development
4 renewable energy
5 Population growth
6 global demand
7 oil shortage

Exercise 2
2 estimate   3 forecasts
4 running out   5 improving

Business communication

Exercise 1
2 I hope we won't have to close the factory.
3 The staff will definitely support the decision.
4 Do you think the strike will be successful?
5 The oil shortage probably won't start until 2015.
6 The world supply of water is unlikely to increase.

Exercise 2
2 likely to find a substitute for oil
3 will probably notice the effects first
4 are likely to rise dramatically
5 definitely won't last forever
6 Hopefully, they'll invest more money

Exercise 3
2 are   3 Hopefully   4 will
5 probably   6 likely

Language at work

Exercise 1
2 We'll finish the report today.
3 The manager may not / might not be in her office right now.
4 Your secretary may / might know when the meeting is.
5 I won't get the job I applied for.
6 They may not / might not give us a pay rise this year.
7 He won't go on any more business trips.

Exercise 2
2 'll be   3 won't feel
4 will exist   5 may/might lose
6 may/might not apply   7 won't find

Unit 14
Working with words

Exercise 1
2 h 3 b 4 d 5 c
6 a 7 e 8 g

Exercise 2
2 enough   3 save   4 time
5 plan   6 schedule   7 allow
8 spend   9 time   10 on time

Business communication

Exercise 1
2 e 3 i 4 c 5 f 6 b
7 h 8 j 9 d 10 g

Exercise 2
1 Oh dear. What's the problem exactly?
2 Basically, I ordered fifty ducks but you sent me chickens.
3 I'm sorry. Would you agree to keep the chickens?
4 No I'm afraid that wouldn't be acceptable.
5 Would it be too late if we sent the ducks today?
6 No, that would allow me to have them for the weekend.
7 OK I'll send them today.

Language at work

Exercise 1
2 didn't know
3 would you think about
4 they would give
5 found themselves
6 they could start
7 might they do
8 could only read
9 we would recommend

Exercise 2
1 had
2 would, had
3 were, would
4 gave, might work
5 would finish, worked
6 Would, sent
7 wouldn't, didn't pay
8 might buy, earned
9 would, didn't get

Practice file answer key

133

Unit 15

Working with words

Exercise 1
2 e   3 f   4 b   5 d
6 c   7 h   8 a

Exercise 2
2 give feedback
3 develop your skills
4 step back
5 set goals
6 motivate
7 achieve
8 improve

Exercise 3
2 motivate
3 give them feedback
4 develop my skills
5 set the goals
6 achieve
7 improve my promotion prospects

Business communication

Exercise 1
2 see
3 worry, a solution
4 Right
5 totally, fault
6 talk, can't
7 thought, contacting, might
8 take, idea

Exercise 2
2 I'm sure there's a solution.
3 Have you thought
4 I can't do that.
5 Why don't
6 That might be possible
7 You could
8 that's a good idea

Language at work

Exercise 1
2 g shouldn't   3 e don't think
4 b could   5 a should
6 c mustn't   7 d must

Exercise 2
2 ✓   3 could   4 mustn't
5 ✓   6 ✓   7 should
8 must

Unit 16

Working with words

Exercise 1
2 d   3 b   4 e   5 f
6 h   7 i   8 a   9 c

Exercise 2
2 concentrate   3 spent
4 give up   5 ambition
6 challenge   7 jobs
8 career   9 complete / finish
10 strength   11 path
12 weakness

Business communication

Exercise 1
2 At the moment
3 Up to now
4 last year
5 Over the next year
6 in my previous role
7 recently

Exercise 2
2 current   3 Recently   4 from
5 Up   6 At   7 future

Exercise 3
2 Up to now
3 Last year
4 at the moment
5 In the future
6 Over the next week

Language at work

Exercise 1
2 didn't stop   3 found
4 has launched   5 has made
6 signed   7 will take
8 is investing   9 hopes

Exercise 2
2 Where shall we advertise
3 Who is going to arrange
4 When are we having
5 How long has he known
6 How much did they pay
7 What time does the last person leave

DVD worksheet answer key

Intercultural communication

1 Answers will vary.

2 1 **Ways of greeting / body language and gesture:** Mihoko comments on how Japanese people bow to each other rather than shake hands or hug.

Level of politeness or formality: Abdullah thinks people in Saudi Arabia are more formal than English people. Dave mentions that in business settings surnames are usually used in France, whereas in the USA first names may be used.

Attitudes towards time: José says that Spanish business people are usually on time for meetings, but that the attitude towards time in social situations with friends and family is less strict and people may well arrive late.

Topics or behaviour that are taboo: David comments on the fact that students need to know this kind of information in a social situation.

Importance of small talk and relationship building before working together: David comments that students will need to know this in a situation where they are having a meeting.

Being direct or indirect: During the lesson, Mihoko explains that Japanese people will complain about a product directly, but not about the service.

2 The topic is complaining. The teacher links this to cultural differences by asking students to discuss the attitudes toward complaining in their countries (i.e. directly or indirectly).

3 David mentions that in business English we refer to two different types of culture: national culture and company culture.

4 Geraldine Gruchet explains that her company has a culture of offering good service to internal staff as well as external customers. The company has to find a balance between the different cultures of the staff working there.

3 Answers will vary, although if you had a student that intended to go to your country, they might appreciate tips and advice as suggested by approach a. Similarly, a list of *dos and don'ts* might be helpful. However, there is sometimes a danger of stereotyping through this kind of approach so it would need to be handled carefully.

4 From what David says in the interview, his approach would probably include b and d.

5 She includes a discussion about complaining and different cultures before stage a. She then follows up stage c with a discussion of how the role plays went in relation to the discussion about cultural differences earlier in the lesson.

6 **Situation 1:** Cultural issues arising out of this might include discussion of what type of greeting is appropriate. For example, do you shake hands? You will also need to draw attention to levels of formality, such as whether to use a person's first name early on in the conversation.

Situation 2: There are two issues here. First of all, the way students talk on the telephone may vary. People from the UK like to make small talk before getting down to business on the phone, whereas someone from Germany may prefer a more direct approach. Negotiating styles also vary from culture to culture. Business people from Asian countries may avoid saying 'no' directly, but someone from North America will be much more direct in the negotiation.

Situation 3: A starting point here will be the question of formality. It is also worth exploring company culture in terms of writing style. Some companies impose strict guidelines for writing letters, so the teacher should ask if students have examples of a company letter. This might include rules on layout and conventions.

Situation 4: This lesson will demonstrate company culture and its approach to applying rules for employees. Students from different cultures may also have different presentation styles that can be very formal and structured or more laid-back and informal.

Meetings

1 Answers will vary.

2 Answers will vary. Possible expressions could be as follows.

Giving an opinion: Personally, I think …

Asking for an opinion: What do you think about …?

Interrupting: Can I just say something here?

Agreeing: I completely agree.

Disagreeing: I'm afraid I don't agree.

Suggesting: Why don't we …?

3 Answers will vary.

4 1 Burcu attended meetings on budgets, schedules, and design issues. Some of these meetings were conference calls.

2 Two kinds meetings: internal and external.

3 We see Judith working on language for *Giving an opinion*, and *Disagreeing*. In the actual lesson she also introduced expressions for *Asking for an opinion, Agreeing,* and *Suggesting*.

5 Answers will vary.

6 1 David refers to the problem of turn-taking. Burcu mentions the problem of having a meeting with native speakers.

2 The advantage of this activity is that it makes students use the new language and helps with turn-taking to some extent. However, it only works as a controlled practice activity and the actual meeting quickly becomes rather inauthentic. Suggestions for activities to help with the other difficulties will vary, although they might include listening to native speakers at natural speed, allowing preparation before a simulated meeting in class, asking students to categorize phrases into informal or formal categories and then to practise using them in appropriate situations, using real teleconference equipment to give students practice in having a meeting without being able to see the other participants.

7 **Approach A:** This is useful where students all come from very different business backgrounds as it would be hard to find a meeting that would be relevant to all. If they have less experience, they might also need some information to support them. Giving the context also means you have some control over what language is used and therefore you can aim for practice of the target language that has been presented in the lesson. The danger is that it can take too long for the students to take in all the information and they may find it hard to put themselves in the situation.

Approach B: This allows you to make the agenda relevant and authentic. However, it relies on all the students knowing something about the items and being able to apply their own experiences. If the agenda is only relevant to a few students, they will talk more and the other students will become de-motivated.

8 1 In this lesson Judith uses approach B for the reasons given above.

2 The students didn't appear to use many expressions taught earlier in the lesson. They started using expressions they already knew. This highlights one disadvantage of eliciting an agenda, rather than giving a topic with information.

3 During the meeting we hear other expressions that are useful for meetings. These include: *That means we have to …, I think …, Maybe the first thing to do is …, First we can … and then secondly we can …*

4 The students in Burcu's group seem to be slightly at odds with one another. The other group appears to be achieving the task quite well. What is also noticeable is that they complete the task using few of the pre-taught expressions.

9 This situation is quite common. Once students have a freer practice activity they will often resort to using language they already know. It is also noticeable that when the task is motivating and relevant, students will focus on the task rather than the language. However, some new expressions will invariably be used by students and the teacher can also discuss phrases that would have helped in the meeting during feedback afterwards.

Self-study

1 Answers will vary.

2 Answers will vary.

3 **Burcu:** do exercises in a text book / grammar book, watch TV / films / DVDs, speak the language with other people

Kevser: do exercises in a text book / grammar book, watch TV / films / DVDs

Geraldine: do exercises in a text book / grammar book, watch TV / films / DVDs, listen to the radio / audio / downloads, speak the language with other people, write to other people in the language

4 Answers will vary.

5 Answers will vary.

6 1 Burcu says it's hard to balance study time with work. In her old job she had to work in the evening so it was difficult to study at home. Geraldine says it's hard because you have to find the time and be very organized (self-disciplined).

2 Because students often use English in their daily work, so they get lots of practice anyway.

7 Answers will vary.

8 David refers to the following: make use of self-study materials provided with a course book (e.g. workbooks).

Cathy refers to the following: set realistic amounts of homework (not too much) with the time they have, advise them to listen to CDs or downloads while waiting in traffic on their way to work, show them how to make use of the Internet or computer-based software for self-study.